This book is to be returned on or before the last date stamped below or you will be charged a fine

New City College – Redbridge campus
Library and Learning Centre
Barley Lane
Romford RM6 4XT

ht͟   ͟irgahosting.com

D1419756

Bonnie and Clyde

Directed by Arthur Penn
Produced by Warren Beatty
Screenplay by David Newman and Robert Benton

Compiled and edited by
Sandra Wake and Nicola Hayden

faber and faber
LONDON · BOSTON

First published in 1972 by Lorrimer Publishing Limited
This edition first published as part of a boxed-set with the
video *Bonnie and Clyde* in 1995 by Faber and Faber Limited
3 Queen Square London WC1N 3AU
Reissued as part of the Classic Screenplay Series in 1998

Printed in England by Clays Ltd, St Ives plc

Original screenplay, dialogue transcript
and photographs of the motion picture based thereon,
© Warner Bros, – Seven Arts, Inc., 1967
This edition of the screenplay © Warner Bros, Inc., 1972

A CIP record for this book is
available from the British Library

ISBN 0–571–19453–2

2 4 6 8 10 9 7 5 3 1

CONTENTS

AN EDITORIAL NOTE

The screenplay of *Bonnie and Clyde* which forms the main part of this volume is based on the original screenplay by David Newman and Robert Benton. In order to make the screenplay correspond as closely as possible to the finished film, the screenplay was checked against a copy of the dialogue continuity and several viewings of the film. The editors, with the help of David Newman and Robert Benton, who in turn consulted with Director Arthur Penn, have incorporated all changes and modifications as they appeared on film, while maintaining the style of the original written form of the screenplay.

The actual production of any film invariably involves some alteration and modification of the original, whether by suggestion of the actors or the director during the day-to-day work, or because of the exigencies of the shooting itself. In this context, the reorganization of three scenes from their place in the original structure to an altered order of appearance, plus the addition of certain lines of dialogue, reflect not only the contributions of the authors, but of Director Arthur Penn, Producer Warren Beatty and Special Consultant Robert Towne as well, not to mention the suggestions of editors, cameramen and fellow workers. Finally, we would like to say that we are indebted to David Newman and Robert Benton, and to Warren Beatty and Arthur Penn for their advice and co-operation in the preparation of *The Bonnie and Clyde Book*.

Arthur Penn

BONNIE AND CLYDE
Private Integrity and Public Violence

From questions at a Press Conference in Montreal 1967
I don't think the original Bonnie and Clyde are very important except insofar as they motivated the writing of a script and our
making of the movie. Whether they are violent or not violent,
whether we are sympathetic to them or not sympathetic, doesn't
matter. They were a part of an event, they were there when it was
happening. So we hung our movie on them, but we don't confine
it to them. This is not a case study of Bonnie and Clyde : we
don't go into them in any kind of depth. They were the outlaws,
they were the sports of nature, they were thrown off by the events
of their day, and they did something about it.

At that time, there was no national police force : they were
all state-confined police forces. When Ford made the V-8, which
was sufficiently powerful to out-run the local police automobiles,
gangs began to spring up. And that was literally the genesis of the
Clyde and Bonnie gang. What happened was that they lived in
their automobile — it was not unusual for them to drive seven and
eight hundred miles in a night, in one of those old automobiles.
They literally spent their lives in the confines of the car. It was
really where they lived. Bonnie wrote her poetry in the car, they
ate ginger snaps in the car, they played checkers in the car — that
was their place of abode. In American Western mythology, the
automobile replaced the horse in terms of the renegade figure.
This was the transformation of the Western into the gangster.

Meanwhile, these very rural people were suffering the terrors
of a depression, which resulted in families being up-rooted, farms
being foreclosed, homes being taken away, by the banks, the
establishment of their world, which in part was represented by
the police. In the context of our film, Bonnie and Clyde found
themselves obliged to fulfil some kind of role which put them in the
position of being folk heroes — violators of the status quo. Retalia-
tors for the people. And, in that context, one finds oneself rooting
for them and, unfortunately, we find ourselves confronted with
the terrible irony that we root for somebody for a relatively good

7

cause who, in the course of that good cause, is called upon to commit acts of violence which repel us.

When a man is in authority — in uniform (I'm now quoting Mack Sennet) it's twice as funny when he slips on a banana peel than when he isn't. And that seems to me to be the essence of what we are dealing with here — which was that violence directed against other people (let us say other people who shared Bonnie and Clyde's given social status) would not be funny — it would not be that hidden Freudian impulse in all of us which is to, somehow, bring the forces of authority at least one rung down the ladder. And if, in this case, Bonnie and Clyde brought them several rungs down the ladder, it was, perforce, funny. It's regrettable that we find it funny, but it's funny. When the President says something rather banal, it's funny. When somebody else says it, it's not very funny.

I don't think it is funny to see the policemen killed, although that doesn't mean there isn't a funny result visible in rather horrible things. I went through a long war, which was rather horrible and funny. There is no question about it : the character of humour in violence is an immediate and constant correlative. They are there, and they are there in almost equal quantities — that was my personal experience. In the film we were attempting to recreate that. The murders get less and less funny, and more and more particular because they begin to be identified with the murderers and, in that sense, we begin to understand the motivation for the murder. The killing gets less impersonal and, consequently, less funny.

With respect to *Bonnie and Clyde* and my other films (*The Left-Handed Gun*, *The Miracle Worker*, *Mickey One*, *The Chase*), I would have to say that I think violence is a part of the American character. It began with the Western, the frontier. America is a country of people who act out their views in violent ways — there is not a strong tradition of persuasion, of ideation, and of law.

Let's face it : Kennedy was shot. We're in Vietnam, shooting people and getting shot. We have not been out of a war for any period of time in my life-time. Gangsters were flourishing during my youth, I was in the war at age 18, then came Korea, now comes Vietnam. We have a violent society. It's not Greece, it's not Athens, it's not the Renaissance — it is the American society, and I would have to personify it by saying that it is a violent one. So why not make films about it.

I don't think one has to make a pre-judgement and say that, because I have strong pacifist tendencies, I must therefore report only pacifist behavior. I think that would be hypocritical. In point of fact, being of a pacifist character or nature perhaps makes me more acutely aware of the character of violence as practiced among human beings, and it somehow interests me more. I find myself drawn to demonstrating it — to dealing with it. Maybe because I'm a coward : I mean, I wouldn't do any of these things — I don't like to fight, but I am intrigued by watching people fight and seeing it happen.

What I meant in *Mickey One,* for instance,, was that we live in a violent time — we make a kind of bargain with violence in our own lifetime. We are in a violent era. And I have to emphasize that I don't mean "violence" only pejoratively. It's violent to get in an airplane and be in Montreal in an hour — it's a violent experience, it's an assault on the senses. It's an assault on the senses to get in an automobile and drive : it's an assault on the senses to do so many of the things that we do. It is the character of the modern world.

I'm getting less interested in the stage and more interested in the cinema. The Broadway stage is designed for a tiny little audience which can afford to pay ten dollars to go to see *How to Succeed in Business.* They consequently, are not a serious audience — one does not do serious work there.

Let's face it, there are no serious plays on Broadway. The so-called serious play has the air of being stately and literary, but it does not really assault any of the fundamental values of its audience. Movies do — they move in on a highly personal level in the way that a book or a poem does. Plays don't do that. If we were dependent upon that audience that goes to Broadway, we would all be disappearing into one little frame of film in about five years — I mean, the theater in New York is disappearing into the musical comedy, and that's it. You go in there, work for six or seven weeks — if the thing is a hit, you get a royalty for the rest of the run. Then you go off and make a movie.

There is a body of history and mythology about Bonnie Parker and Clyde Barrow which includes various estimates of their sexuality. We chose, among other things, the characteristic of *relative* impotence in Clyde as a condition not dissimilar from what my personal sense is of what their life was like in that period in the Southwest. It's a peculiarly puritanical society — a peculiarly rigid, moralistic society — and we were trying to distinguish between the rigid morality which could very well render somebody impotent at the interior, private level while at the same time he could exceed all limits of external morality and still feel at one with himself. It seems to me not too uncharacteristic of some of the things that are visible in the south of the United States today: a church-going, highly moralistic, highly puritanical society, which has integrated and made a part of itself a kind of violence against other human beings, which, viewed from the outside, seems absolutely intolerable. It was that kind of disparity — between a private integrity and a public violence — which we were trying to delineate in the film.

David Newman and Robert Benton

LIGHTNING IN A BOTTLE

We must have heard the expression a thousand times by now:
"You guys caught lightning in a bottle with that one." It has
emerged from the mouths of studio executives, producers, agents,
even aunts and uncles — always that same damned phrase about
"lightning in a bottle" and often with the implied hope that we
might somehow pull that trick off again. In retrospect, it seems
a pretty accurate summary of what happened when you consider
not only the success of the movie itself, but all the incredible
stuff that followed: the fashion fad, the newspaper editorials, the
hit songs, the cover stories, the satires, the posters, the amateur
robberies "in the style of", and the pleasant, slightly spooky feeling
of having coined three household words (if you include the "and").
But there were quite a few years before all that came to pass when
we never stopped to think about the lightning at all. We were
just trying to sell the bottle.

In 1964 we had both been working for *Esquire Magazine* for a
few years as an editor and art director respectively. By then most
of our official working time was spent conjuring up and executing
"features" for the publication, but in fact what we were mostly
doing was talking about movies. What the Managing Editor didn't
know didn't hurt him; as long as he saw us in conference, he
assumed we were doing our job. At that time, like a million of you,
we were riding the crest of the new wave that had swept in on our
minds, and the talk was Truffaut, Godard, De Broca, Bergman,
Kurosawa, Antonioni, Fellini and all the other names that fell
like a litany in 1964, along with sudden and staggering highs of
rediscovery and personal prejudice around the pantheon people —
Hitchcock, Hawks, Ford, Welles and the rest. Not just credits to us,
to two who spent their childhoods two thousand miles apart but
panting in unison at the same Martha Vickers pout, the same
cattle drive, the same dream of being a part of it, somehow, getting
in on it. Our minds most recently blown by *Breathless*, we
addressed ourselves more and more, during working hours and
drinking hours, to the idea of actually doing something about it.
And the first idea, the very first one, was a movie about two Texas

13

desperadoes named Bonnie Parker and Clyde Barrow.

Three factors conspired in the creation. With no particular end in mind, we began noticing reactions around us that, however intangible, seemed to fall into some sort of pattern. At first we weren't sure this pattern was going to emerge as something clear enough to make a statement about; we were sure, though, that everything we discussed, thought about, and felt could be looked at in this light. This pattern became our primary reference for weeks on end and eventually it became an *Esquire* piece called *The New Sentimentality*.

The article appeared in June 1964 and struck a nerve. A lot of response, a lot of identification, a lot of interesting letters continuing the notion. What had been our own bull-session appeared to have some kind of real relevance to readers, and, in addition, we kept developing it for ourselves. What we had, although we didn't consciously think of it at the time, was a set of ideas in search of a movie.

At which point, a writer named John Toland published a book called *The Dillinger Days,* a fascinating history of the notorious Dillinger gang with side-trips and footnotes concerning their contemporaries — Ma Barker, Machine Gun Kelly, Baby Face Nelson, Bonnie and Clyde. The material on the Barrows was slight, really, but there was something about these people, this blonde girl who wrote Robert Service-style doggerel poetry, this feeling we had of a bizarre "professional love affair", the time and the place — all of it made us think, "It's a movie." A New Sentimentality movie.

The third contributing factor to the genesis was an Alfred Hitchcock retrospective at the Museum of Modern Art in New York. Every day for over a month, we sat in the MOMA auditorium and watched the great man's *oeuvre* from silents to the latest, and we came away each time babbling, excited, thoroughly converted believers. It was an education in pure cinema — any one of the films contains the grammar, the techniques, the art and the vision — and the result was that by the time the series was drawing to a close, we *had* to make movies the way one *has* to breathe. *Bonnie and Clyde* is loaded with its influences, and some may be more apparent than Hitchcock, but there wasn't a day spent in the writing that didn't include at least one discussion on

14

what *he* would have done.

Well, here we were: an idea for a movie, a love of movies, a sense of the kind of picture we wanted to write and absolutely no knowledge at all of the movie *business*. In the same spirit of amateurism, we turned to two friends who thought it would be exciting to produce one. They knew a little more about it than we did, but not much. "The thing to do," they counseled, "is write a treatment first and then we can get backing."

After nine years in this business, we can state with some authority that nobody knows exactly what a treatment is. Some producers want one, some don't. Some mean an outline of the plot, maybe ten or fifteen pages. Some mean a sort of "presentation" of the idea, two or three pages. And some mean what we took it to mean; our "treatment" was, in effect, a full shooting script minus the dialogue, seventy pages long, including cuts, dissolves, key camera set-ups, even music cues. We worked on it at night, every night, with a Mercury record of Flatt and Scruggs and the Foggy Mountain Boys doing *Foggy Mountain Breakdown* loud in the background, and that tune seemed to contain the essence of what we wanted. Happily, it wound up being most of the musical sound-track of the picture when it was discovered that the world contained no banjo player, no matter how expert, who could pick with that same lightning-fast drive as Earl Scruggs.

Perhaps the heaviest influence on our heads as we wrote was Truffaut, especially two films: *Shoot the Piano Player,* with its wonderful combination of comedy and bleakness, gangsterism and humanity, and *Jules and Jim,* which managed to define the present as it evoked the past; their spirit informed us as we wrote. And so, for a couple of guys who knew next to nothing about how such things *should* be done, it seemed quite natural to try and interest François Truffaut in directing *Bonnie and Clyde.* Had we been more sophisticated about this business, we never would have had the *chutzpah* to try. But try we did, and it turned out to be the best thing we could have done.

Both of us knew, professionally, an extraordinary woman named Helen Scott who ran the French Film Office in New York and was a great help to magazine editors in setting up interviews, providing stills and even translating when a visiting dignitary came to New York. Helen, we knew, was (still is) very close to

15

Truffaut and the other young French film makers. She informed us that it was her policy to never, absolutely never read ideas submitted for Truffaut (it seems we were not the first to try) but that as a favor to us, she would read our treatment.

She did more than that. She called us back, highly excited by what she had read, and said that this time she would break her own rule and send it to Truffaut with her own recommendation. If ever there was a good argument for doing the kind of long and detailed treatment we did, it is in this instance. Our treatment, in addition to the scene-by-scene breakdown of the film, also contained a lot of what we thought the film was "about". Critics have had so many field days on that particular subject since the film opened that they add up to a field year; it might be useful at this point, then, to say a few words on what we, its writers, think it's "about."

It is about style and people who have style. It is about people whose style set them apart from their time and place so that they seemed odd and aberrant to the general run of society. It should be borne in mind that, in our version of their lives, it isn't the robbing of banks or even the killing of peace officers that made Bonnie and Clyde such pariahs. No, a lot of poor people in those depressed years could identify with those activities, even enjoy them vicariously. It was the aberrations of social style, however, that got the population's dander up : Bonnie's poetry which she persistently sent into the papers to see it in print, for example. What kind of thing was that for a gangster to do? And then the business with Bonnie smoking cigars. Although she claimed she had done it once and for a gag, it was the singlemost salient prop in her career, the thing the public remembered and remarked upon. We put the business of C. W. Moss's tattoo in the film for exactly this reason; his father cares not a whit about his son turning criminal, but those "pictures on his skin" really outrage his sensibilities. The tattoo, as much as anything, causes him to participate in the final ambush.

And then there was the incredible narcissism of Bonnie and Clyde. They never got rich, and, as the film shows, never really expected to. But they *did* get to be celebrities, and they loved it. This business of constantly taking photographs and mailing them to the newspapers was a key (to us) to the characters of Bonnie and Clyde, a predeliction that seemed truer than ever in the 60's when our culture was creating a new set of "instant celebrities," people who became famous by doing nothing except acting famous. The love that we imagined to exist between Bonnie and Clyde was what we called "a professional love affair" between two people who sensed each other's needs, who provided, in effect, a mirror for each other. In recent years, since the movie opened, critics and interviewers have told us that *Bonnie and Clyde* was *really* about Vietnam, *really* about police brutality, *really* about Lee Harvey Oswald, *really* about Watts. After a while, we took to shrugging and saying, "If you think so." But to us, it is *really* about those facets of American sensibility we mentioned in *The New Sentimentality*, and about what was contained in a short introduction we provided in the treatment before we sent it off to Truffaut. This is what we wrote then :

"A Few Notes About This Movie. In the early 1930's America saw (and enjoyed) a revival of crime and criminal style that it had last seen in the wild west : the time of the desperado. The organized crime that had functioned so well in the 20's was so *well* organized that it was Business — a matter of lawyers, managers, syndicates, graft and corruption. The big criminals — Capone, Moran etc. — were businessmen.

"But with the Depression and the end of prohibition came a different type of crime and criminal, the wild, colorful and very unbusinesslike desperadoes. In many ways, their origins were similar. All had their heyday in the southwest and the midwest, areas hit hard by the times. They came not from criminal societies but from poor backgrounds. They did not form organizations. Instead, they had little gangs, no bigger than five or six, and they ran from place to place executing daring robberies, knocking over banks, stores, gas stations, living from day to day, killing at random. And they killed often.

"A few factors contributed to their flourishing. First, there were fast cars, and there never had been such fast cars before, cars that could do up to 90 mph. And so these southwest bandits replaced the horses of Jesse James and Billy the Kid with Fords, LaSalles and Plymouths. But otherwise, their style was the same.

"But the cars wouldn't have been much good without the roads. The early 30's brought the interstate highways to America. Smooth roads that were designed to keep things moving swiftly.

Fast cars and fast roads to drive on — a bandit could rob a bank in one state, drive like hell, and be two hundred miles away from the scene of the crime by night.

"The reason the lawlessness could flourish under these conditions was augmented by the fact that American law enforcement had not kept pace with technology. Though a man could travel from one state to another, the police could not travel with him. At that point state law enforcement ended at the state line, and pursuit ended with it. If a man killed in Kansas and escaped to Oklahoma, it was up to the Oklahoma police to pick up the chase.

"By the middle of the 30's the situation had been corrected, but in the early part of the decade it was easier to make a getaway, easier to hide, easier to dodge, easier to move around.

"Bonnie Parker and Clyde Barrow headed one of the notorious gangs, and their names and deeds were well-known across the country. To many they were heroes of a kind, for they showed bravery in the face of incredible odds, daring in their free enterprise, and style in their manner. They took a delight, it seemed, in foiling the law — the small town cops, the sheriffs, the justices of the peace. For many decent citizens, there was a vicarious thrill in that, for these were the same people who busted strikes, pushed bread lines, ticketed caravans and, in general, seemed to represent oppressive authority at a time when everything was tough for everyone.

"Bonnie and Clyde were so well-known and even revered in Texas and the surrounding areas that children would go to costume parties dressed up as the notorious pair. Their exploits became legend, and naturally they were exaggerated by many. Untold killings and robberies were ascribed to them which they didn't commit. But, of course, that was tribute of a kind.

"By the time their careers ended, they had achieved an almost supernatural status in the eyes of many newspaper readers. For how could a little blonde girl and her man escape so many rugged lawmen, time and time again?

"They were folk heroes, and though their defeat was wished (that was, after all, a part of American lore — that the bad guys be as fascinating and marvelous as could be for a while, but that ultimately the good guys must win) their career was followed with interest by millions at the time.

18

"That is the background of this film, insofar as its relation to crime in regional America is concerned. There is another point to make, however.

"Bonnie and Clyde were out of their time in the 30's. They represented 'the underworld' (a word heard less and less today) and that term embraced an entire concept of underworld mores, habits, jargon, style, codes, loyalties and methods which were, to the average American, exotic and foreign. Today, in a time when everybody likes to talk about being 'aware,' we have inherited a legacy from that underworld. What we now call 'the underground,' what the hip people do and are and feel, stems in great part from that 'underworld.'

"If Bonnie and Clyde were here today, they would be hip. Their values have become assimilated in much of our culture — not robbing banks and killing people, of course, but their style, their sexuality, their bravado, their delicacy, their cultivated arrogance, their narcissistic insecurity, their curious ambition have relevance to the way we live now.

"Of course, what makes them beautiful is that they didn't know it. They knew they had something to say, but they went about it in a way which inevitably brought doom. But even in the light of their brief lives, we can see they were not squares. Al Capone, he was a square. Clyde Barrow, no.

"This is a movie about criminals only incidentally. Crime in the 30's was the strange, the exotic, the different. This is a movie about two people, lovers, movers and operators. They were 'hung up,' like many people are today. They moved in odd, unpredictable ways which can be viewed, with an existential eye, as classic. Their relationship, in fact, is an existential one. Their crimes were against man, and their best moments came because of their commitment to their own humanity.

"They are not Crooks. They are people, and this film is, in many ways, about what's going on now."

End of Introduction, with belated apologies for the touch of pomposity that creeps in toward the end. But so it was, and so it went to Truffaut. Before we finished it, we had spent days in the library, reading up on everything we could find from old newspapers to true detective magazines. We had written to Dallas papers and police sources for further elucidation. We had groaned under the weight of the research and groaned with despair as we had to make the decisions to throw out some wonderful factual material, Clyde's saxophone-playing hobby, for instance, because it was "too much." We had decided early on that, for dramatic purposes, certain figures of considerable importance in the true history had to be eliminated, certain adventures altered or dropped, certain facts ignored and certain legends adhered to, certain characters combined from many into one for the sake of simplification, as in C. W. Moss who was actually a conglomeration of four different side-kicks in the history of the Barrow Gang. Neither of us had been born when Bonnie and Clyde were ambushed; but we were beginning to feel we'd lived through it all.

One month later, François Truffaut arrived in New York with our treatment translated into French, a document that may not seem very important to the rest of the world but convinced us at first look that we would stay in movies for the rest of our lives. With Helen Scott functioning as speed-demon translator, Truffaut sat with us in his room at the Hotel Drake for three days and gave us, first, his enthusiasm, second, his knowledge, and third, his problems in scheduling. About the first, it is enough to say that we will never forget it.

The second provided us with an invaluable education in the art of cinema. Truffaut had broken the treatment down into what he called "unities," i.e. blocks of the film which stood as emotional and dramatic entities. By structuring it that way, he demonstrated to us the difference between "real time" and "film time," pointing out where we had goofed somewhat in sacrificing the emotional curves of the film for factual or actual purposes. He indicated areas that could be tightened, and he realized for us one of the *schemas* in the treatment that was already there not wholly by our conscious design—that Bonnie and Clyde were most vulnerable when they were most ordinarily human. When engaged in bank robbing and the like, they handled situations fairly well, give or take complications. But when they chose to settle down and behave like regular folks, setting up house-keeping in Joplin, for example, *then* the laws would find them and blast them back into a life on the run. He gave us one or two specifics, such as the device of tying time together in film terms during Bonnie's reading of "The Ballad of Bonnie and Clyde" by going from Bonnie reading from her notebook, to Hamer at his desk reading it in the newspaper, to Bonnie and Clyde reading the last verses as published. But really his suggestions were all of a theoretical sort as to make us aware of what we might do to sharpen it and better it. He also thought it a good idea for us all to screen a few movies that seemed relevant, which is why one evening we found ourselves in a projection room looking at Joseph Lewis's *Gun Crazy*, a film based on the Bonnie and Clyde legend, because Truffaut felt that its ending was too drawn-out and predictable. Another visiting French director sat in the back row that night and didn't have too much to say; but it was enough for us simply to meet him — Jean-Luc Godard.

As for Truffaut's problems, they were twofold. First, his schedule: for a few years now he had very much wanted to make a movie of Ray Bradbury's *Fahrenheit 451*. The financing had been waxing and waning, at the moment waning, but should it come through, he would have to devote himself to *Fahrenheit* and wouldn't be able to do *Bonnie and Clyde*. (At that time, Truffaut had organized his life along the pattern of doing one picture a year and never planning beyond that; he has since become more prolific and less rigorous about scheduling.) The second problem was language — he spoke no English at all (which would be a problem with *Fahrenheit* as well) and knew very little about the part of the country where *Bonnie and Clyde* would be filmed. This seemed an advantage to us at the time; we felt that the exoticism of the material, which even to us — one New Yorker for whom Texas was as foreign and colorful as Timbuktu and one Texan for whom the idea that the very innocent streets on which he had spent his childhood were once the scene of gun battles and chases was fantasy in the extreme — would be enhanced by a Frenchman's vision of America in the Thirties. At the time, we felt he would "see" things an American wouldn't, along the lines of Nabokov doing the American motels in *Lolita* better than any native could have done. We have since been told, by Truffaut among others, that we were wrong to think so and events have certainly borne this out, but at the time it seemed like a good idea.

Truffaut left, we got a leave of absence from our jobs and decided it was time to go to East Texas and really get into it. We had, by then, a contract with our friends and they put out enough money for train tickets. Our reasons for going were many: first, to

21

scout locations for the film; second, to find people who actually knew the real Bonnie and Clyde; third, to listen to the language patterns, the speech cadences, the colloquialisms, so as to insure absolute accuracy in the dialogue. In addition, we wanted to hear as many Texas dialects as possible, since it wasn't enough that each character should sound like Texas, but that each spoke with a voice distinct from the others.

The Texas trip was a delight. We found little towns near Dallas that had been bypassed by the highways and looked exactly as they did in the era of Bonnie and Clyde, towns named Venus, Midlothian, Denton and Pilot's Point. We found cornfields and meadows and gas stations which fitted right in, and we took pictures of everything. We met a lawman who had been there when the bodies were brought in and remembered the bullet holes in the car. We met a West Dallas body shop owner who had gone to school with Clyde and told us. "They wasn't nothin' bad about them two; it was the newspapers that done 'em in." We met a woman who had taught Clyde in third grade and recalled that he used to throw rocks at her when she came to school. We spent a memorable afternoon with two old ladies in Waxahachie, Texas, Miss Mabel and Miss Eva Grizzard (we used their name for the character of the undertaker) who told us the joke about the man who put whiskey in his sick mother's milk, the joke that became, word for word, Buck's "Don't sell that cow!" story. We spoke to a retired judge who remembered the notorious pair as "just trash" and a woman who said that when she was a girl, Bonnie and Clyde stopped at a poor farmer's house and left free groceries. We spent an entire day scouring around an abandoned graveyard in West Dallas searching for the graves of Clyde and Buck and finally found them side by side in a remote corner, covered by weeds. We cleaned them off and read the faded inscription, "Gone But Not Forgotten." Not by us, anyway. We also found Bonnie's grave, this time in a well-kept cemetery near Love Field where the manager told us that people came all the time looking for Bonnie's resting place, and that the FBI kept an open file on the Parker family to this day. And you can bet we took a picture of the bronze plaque that marked the site, which has the following poem by Bonnie Parker:
"As the flowers are made sweeter
By the sunshine and the dew,

So this world is made much brighter
By the likes of folks like you."

We came back to New York and wrote the screenplay, and then sent it, along with all the photographs, to François Truffaut. And then we waited.

A month went by, we went back to work, and then came a letter from Paris. He had liked it quite a lot, he said, but the trouble was that the *Fahrenheit* financing had come through after all, so it looked like he couldn't do it. However, he had "taken the liberty of passing it on to Jean-Luc Godard." It was a remarkable letter, because we were plunged to the depths by the third paragraph and then rocketed to the sky by the sign-off. Godard was, if anything, the only film-maker in the world who excited as much as Truffaut at that moment in time. We had seen and endlessly discussed all his films, which had been coming out at the rate of every other month, it seemed. Each one a revelation, each one a re-definition of the limits of cinema, each one cause for reconsidering every idea about movies we had ever had, each one a major work. A few days later came a cable; Godard was coming to New York and would call us.

For our producers, however, the idea of Godard didn't sit quite as comfortably as Truffaut. We attempted to quiet their fears, even bully them into our enthusiasm. By the time Godard showed, they were willing to see what happened, if (understandably) nervous about a director who had the reputation of (a) making movies in three weeks and (b) never having worked from a script in his entire career.

Once again the ever-helpful Helen Scott was present, but the meeting between all of us—producers, writers and Godard — remains more risible in her memory than in ours. Godard was everything we had heard — mercurial, impulsive, rash, brilliant. What it boiled down to was this : he had been supposed to start another film in Paris next month, but he didn't feel much like doing it. He liked the script for *Bonnie and Clyde* very much and thought he would do that. In three weeks from now.

Our producers went white. But, they said, we were not ready, that is, there was no deal, no financing, no studio. Godard said it didn't matter; we immediately agreed with him. Why not? He said, that day, two things which are forever writ upon our memories: "If it happens in life, it can happen in a movie." This to the producer's objection that the key elements might not be perfectly pulled together in three weeks time. And, "We can make this film anywhere; we can make it in Tokyo." This in response to the producers' objection that weather conditions were not right in Texas for shooting at this time of year. A call to the weather bureau in Dallas was made. Strong possibilities of precipitation were predicted. "You see?" said the producer.

"I am speaking cinema and you are speaking meteorology," said Godard.

Whatever the problems, we two were ready to commit anything to him under any conditions to go ahead. Make it Tokyo, so what, it'll be great. And in its own way, it surely would have been. But there was no moving the producers, who were understandably caught short, especially in the area of financing, and there was no *détente* that could be made between them and Godard, in spite of our pleas. The next day we met him for a drink at his hotel. "Call me when the script reverts to your ownership," said he. An hour later he was on the plane back to Paris and the pre-production of *Alphaville*.

At this point, an emotion that can only be accurately described as total despair set in. We had this script. We had, fortunately, this contract which contained very little cash in it but two important clauses — that of director approval and that of the producers' option expiring in eighteen months, at which point the script reverted to our ownership.

A month of miasma passed, at the end of which we submitted a heady list of directors to our producers and they submitted another one to us; disagreement was rife. We were still on our European kick, with a few exceptions of American super-directors for whom the likelihood of making our film was largely out of the question for reasons of schedule and/or sympathy to the material. One of the few Americans we did seek out, however, was Arthur Penn. Before we could even submit the script, we learned from his office that his schedule was full. And the months dragged on, with flickers of interest from sources uninteresting to us, rejections from people we never thought would say yes in the first place, and the slow, sinking feeling that all was lost. *Bonnie and Clyde* went into a drawer.

24

We didn't, however. We left *Esquire* and free-lanced magazine articles. We wrote a Broadway musical about Superman, imbuing the hero with a lot of our Bonnie and Clyde notions; we saw in the double life of Clark Kent/Superman a kind of caped Clyde. It got fine reviews and flopped in less than four months. We wrote a book. And we got more rejections every time the script came out of the drawer. At one point, for one brief shining moment, Truffaut suddenly became available again. The "package" (script and director) went to almost every major studio in the country (for some reason, however, never to Warner Bros., who finally made it), and some not-so-major. Without exception, it was turned down by all, with comments that we still keep locked in a secret file to warm ourselves by on cold nights. The comments were all along the lines of, "Who could care less about characters like these? They are repulsive people. The package is too exotic. Who's Truffaut to make an American gangster movie? Why would anybody want to see a story like this?" And so on, culminating in a meeting with a tyro New York producer-financer who told us he might be interested in it if we changed the characters to "the real animals they were. You've got to lift up the manhole of this sewer and let us smell the stench," said he, as we backed rapidly out of his office.

Once in a while, somebody in the business would call and say they'd "seen it" around, and liked it, and whatever happened to it, anyway? We consoled ourselves with work, family and small vices. Our producers, who were trying to the best of their ability to get the project going and who never lost faith, mirrored our depression. All was lost. Maybe the next one, huh. . . .

Towards the end of that eighteen months, an American actor named Warren Beatty met, socially, a French director named François Truffaut in Paris. Truffaut mentioned to him that he had read a script that Beatty might be interested in, that there was a very good part in it for him. Warren called us ("Hey! It's Warren Beatty! The movie star! On the phone!") and asked to read it. We explained that it was under option to our producers; he said he wanted to read it, anyway. He picked it up that night, and the next morning we got the second call. It was the kind we'd thought would never come; he had only read half of it so far, but already knew that he wanted to do it. However, he wanted to produce it as well. He would wait out the option. We kissed our wives and broke open a fresh six-pack and started playing Flatt and Scruggs again.

The day Warren purchased the script — the day after the old option lapsed — we met and discussed directors. He had granted us the same approval contractually; in addition, he wanted our close involvement at all times. He got it. Names came up, and Warren immediately put forth Arthur Penn. Tried and failed, we explained. "Don't worry," he said, "If I have to, I'll lock myself in a room with him and I won't let him out until he says yes."

We were all for that, but at the same time pointed out the old Godard interest. Warren was skeptical. The next day came a cable from Godard inquiring about the situation. Some weeks later there took place in a hotel room in London an historic meeting between Warren Beatty and Jean-Luc Godard; one of them was sick with a fever, but we forget which one. In any case, by the end of it, apparently, it could have been either or both. We've often speculated, sometimes with Godard, what *Bonnie and Clyde* would have been had he directed it; certainly it wouldn't have been the picture the world now knows and certainly it wouldn't have been the picture we had in mind, but it would have been something of its own, probably not unlike *Pierrot Le Fou,* and certainly fascinating.

Back in New York now, Arthur Penn, without even the locked room technique, read the script and said yes. We drove out to his home in Stockbridge, Massachusetts for the first of what were to be many meetings.

If there is one thing we have learned beyond any question in the movie business, it is this : once there is a director, he is the boss. The absolute boss. And so it should be, at least in theory, because if he's good the picture will profit. If he's not, then you're stuck with a lousy director. There are those, too. But there can be only one general, in spite of all the theories advanced by non-directors promulgating the notion of "film-making by committee." Certainly there *is* a group effort, but it all must pass muster with the boss, for it is his job to put all those elements together into one functioning whole. Ultimately *his* vision becomes the primary one. *Always,* the worth of the final picture stands or falls on his ability.

The halls of the Writers Guild have rung for decades with the anguished cries of screenwriters concerning the directors who, "butchered the screenplay." Sometimes the charge is true. But if you get lucky, you find a director who understands what you saw and what you intended, who reacts to the best of the work in exactly the way you hoped he might, who searches out the flaws and weaknesses and suggests the way to fix them. That's if you're lucky. If you are Very Lucky, you get Arthur Penn.

From the moment Penn agreed to direct *Bonnie and Clyde,* we knew that it was, in a sense, no longer our baby. We approached the first conference with trepidation; we came away more excited than we had been in two years. Arthur's contribution to the picture, even on the structuring and re-writing level, was incalculable. He reeled off, for openers, the things he loved in the first draft and the particular delight he found in the bizarre combination of humor and harrowing violence, the one butted up against the other. We talked a lot about the violence, about the idea that, simple as it may sound, "bullets should hurt when they go in people and the audience should feel that hurt." Arthur also discussed the elements he felt needed shoring up in the next draft — much more sense of the time being a period of vast social and economic chaos. He remembered the Depression; we didn't. We talked about that, and where to increase its effect on the lives of our characters, how to show them in stronger relief against the background of economic upheaval. The sequence with the farmer who helps shoot out his windows, for example, came out of that first discussion.

Another aspect of the movie that Arthur wanted to stress even more than we had — and we thought we had done a lot of it — was the legendary quality, the myth of Bonnie and Clyde as two magic people whose reverberations, even in their own lifetime, touched deeply the secret fantasies of average Americans.

And then there was the sex problem. In all our research on Clyde Barrow, we had come across veiled and often contradictory references to Clyde's sex life. All the sources indicated it wasn't quite "normal," but many left it at that. Some inferred an S-M trip. More inferred homosexuality, and one or two ventured the thought that Clyde and Bonnie and one or another of the various men in the gang at different times were involved in a functioning *ménage-à-trois,* a mini-orgy in every little motel. We liked that idea; it seemed just bizarre and somehow brave enough to fit right in with our notion of the Barrow Gang's avant-garde style. And

27

so the first draft contained an on-going sexual relationship between Bonnie, Clyde, and C. W. Moss; we had our Bonnie in love with Clyde, to be sure, but our Clyde, while in love with Bonnie, unable to perform sexually without the stimulation of the third (generally) unwilling sidekick. Bear in mind, *please,* that C.W. at that time was not at all the character that Michael J. Pollard played in the movie. In this first version, he was a kind of dumb stud, simple and sweet.

Arthur didn't go for it, and it worried Warren, too. The problem, as we hassled it over, boiled down to this; once you label your hero as a sexual deviant, no matter how much you stress his emotional love for the heroine, no matter how little film time you give to that aspect of him, it colors the character forevermore in the minds of the audience. Worse, it turns them off. Every other action he performs can be written off by offended patrons as "Well, sure, the guy's a pervert, whatd'ya expect." And clearly that was not our intention; in fact, it was destructive in the extreme. We also began to realize that we didn't know the first thing in the world about what living in a practising *ménage-à-trois* was really like — how its psychic vibrations would affect the characters in their daily lives, for example. We had just ignored that in our quest for an off-beat love affair.

Oddly enough, the minute we agreed to take it out, we were immensely relieved. It had always been bothersome, but we'd kept the bother in the background. Arthur did agree, however, that *some* sexual problem was vital for the dynamics of the character and the relationship; for just as their dreams of being the golden couple were constantly coming up against the reality of the deadly days, so too was the resolution of their "togetherness" to reflect that strain. And the marriage proposal scene, in bed, toward the end of the picture, *was* already in the script and we all wanted to keep that word for word. But what to build toward it with? Well . . . we tabled it.

The idea of Clyde's impotence didn't come immediately. We sat with Arthur and psyched Clyde out backwards, so to speak, eliminating by both common and psychological sense all the other "problems" that came to mind, so that the correctness of impotence, given this character, this world and this love affair, made itself known by process of elimination. And once we had it, we knew it

28

was right, even Warren Beatty who, to his credit, joked only once about what it would do to "his image" and then never worried about it again. Even more, he began to think of ways to bolster the notion in his portrayal.

In the months that followed, both in Stockbridge and later in Los Angeles, the meetings, and the new pages, kept coming. We learned from Arthur a term that has since gone into our working vocabulary: "the profile" of a film. He would sit at his desk, feet up in Burbank, and stare at sheets of yellow legal paper tacked on the wall. For hours, he would do this, silent. We looked at the paper; it had every scene in the script (whatever stage the script was in that day) listed. That was all. And finally, he would look up and say something like, "The profile isn't right. It sags between numbers 10 and 14." A profile was, simply, the dramatic curve of the picture, and one of Arthur's great talents is to "see" the picture in his mind before it gets before the camera and realize that the tension abates too much in one section, or that some sequence is just too long to make its point. Or perhaps the laughs come bunched together for ten minutes here when we need some of them there. Sometimes it took a deal of convincing on his part, and a few times we reconvinced him. But in general there was agreement, with Warren Beatty actively involved, and often the solution turned out to be as simple a matter as taking two scenes and switching them around. Suddenly the profile would tighten. We did our share of crying, half out of conviction and half out of tradition, when some little line or piece of business we cherished was chopped off. But by the time the picture was ready to shoot —and the adjustments had been made to the casting, i.e. having come up with the idea of Michael J. Pollard, the character of C.W. underwent many changes with that wonderfully quirky actor in mind — it was the film we *all* wanted to make, the film Arthur Penn *did* make. What touches, slight alterations, and fixes occurred during the shooting and the editing, which we followed with more than average interest and increasing happiness, were the result of Arthur's knowledge of what he was going to do so well that he could afford to play around a little when there seemed to be a flash of inspiration. Some of that never made it to the screen, some did. But when we, the writers, were asked later whether *Bonnie and Clyde* turned out to be the picture we meant it to be, we had

29

no hesitation in answering affirmatively.

Some people bristle at the idea of collaboration. But we had been doing it ourselves for a few years now and had learned the give and take routine and its benefits. The addition of a director and a producer who had ideas of their own to contribute — the normal movie situation, by the way — did not come as a shock to us, then. And since it was *good* collaborating, it spurred us on to make things better. "Everything that happens from now on," said Warren, "is for the good of the picture." He was to exemplify that by truly practicing what he preached at every stage of the game, right down to visiting the projection booths when the picture opened in major cities and adjusting the sound level before the eyes of unbelieving projectionists.

Our cinematic virginity had been taken in the most memorable way, as everything that happened afterwards was to demonstrate. The rest is not only history but, for us, memories — the Paris opening where everywhere we went were Bonnie and Clyde clothes, songs, posters, culminating in a tacky-wonderful drive to the premiere in vintage automobiles and that great minute when all the photographers started taking our pictures until they realized that Warren Beatty and Faye Dunaway were in the *next* car and we suddenly found ourselves abandoned and alone, laughing like maniacs, our wives the only ones who cared to stay with the writers. And the awards, a lot of them, which got us to Oscar night and a lot of studio folks saying, "In the bag, boys. (We were always "the boys" around there; used to hate it, now, graying, we miss it a little). Got your speeches ready?"

No, we said. (We did have them, though.) And then *didn't* win it and somehow restrained ourselves from tackling the guy who did as he bounded down the aisle with the statuette.

And finally standing on a beach one day, toeing sand and kicking abstractedly at the surf, and slowly, slowly beginning to talk about what would the next one be. We were feeling like veterans then, old pros even, with plaques and interviews and reviews and "think pieces" filling up the files. We talked about a new idea, but never even dared to look down at that bottle the tide had just washed in at our feet, because we knew there wouldn't be any lightning in it and there never is if you go looking for it. Sometimes, though, it happens.

BONNIE AND CLYDE

Screenplay by

David Newman & Robert Benton

CREDITS :

Screenplay by — David Newman and Robert Benton
Directed by — Arthur Penn
Produced by — Warren Beatty
Production Company — Tatira-Hiller Productions
Music Composed by — Charles Strouse
"Foggy Mountain Breakdown" — Flatt & Scruggs, courtesy of Mercury Records

Director of Photography — Burnett Guffey, A.S.C.
Art Director — Dean Tavoularis
Edited by — Dede Allen
Costumes — Theadora van Runkle
Special Consultant — Robert Towne
Assistant to the Producer — Elaine Michea
Assistant Director — Jack N. Reddish
Production Manager — Russ Saunders
Script Supervisor — John Dutton
Sound by — Francis E. Stahl
Set Decorator — Raymond Paul
Make-up — Robert Juras
Special Effects — Danny Lee
Hair Stylist — Gladys Witten
Miss Dunaway's Make-up — Warner Bros. Cosmetics
Men's Wardrobe — Andy Matyasi
Women's Wardrobe — Norma Brown
Process — Technicolor
Running Time — 111 minutes
Distributed in the United States and Great Britain
by Warner Bros. - Seven Arts Inc.

CAST :

Clyde Barrow	Warren Beatty
Bonnie Parker	Faye Dunaway
C. W. Moss	Michael J. Pollard
Buck Barrow	Gene Hackman
Blanche	Estelle Parsons
Frank Hamer	Denver Pyle
Malcolm Moss	Dub Taylor
Velma Davis	Evans Evans
Eugene Grizzard	Gene Wilder

CAST OF CHARACTERS

This is the original list of characters which David Newman and Robert Benton included in their original screenplay. One or two characters were left out of the final film and other characters were changed or modified by the actors who finally played the parts.

CLYDE BARROW : Young, dapper, reckless.

BONNIE PARKER : Blonde, somewhat fragile, intelligent in expression.

C. W. MOSS : 1931 version of a rock 'n' roll hood; blond, surly, and not very bright.

BUCK BARROW : Clyde's older brother, a chubby, jovial, simple, big-hearted man.

BLANCHE : Buck's wife; a young housefrau, no more no less, inclined to panic.

SHERIFF FRANK HAMER : Tall, strong, contemptuous of almost everyone and particularly women and criminals; some hidden evil in him sometimes shows in his face.

MALCOLM MOSS : C.W.'s father; a fat farmer with gray hair, shrewd and cunning.

BONNIE'S MOTHER : A fragile, weepy woman.

BONNIE'S SISTER

BONNIE'S UNCLE

EUGENE GRIZZARD : A Texas undertaker, about 30 years old.

VELMA DAVIS : Grizzard's sweetheart, a little younger.

MR. WEEKS : A real estate agent in Joplin, Missouri.

GROCERY DELIVERY BOY : In Joplin.

HAWKINS : A Missouri bank guard.

BANK CUSTOMER : A snooty, middle-aged matron.

TATTOO ARTIST : Skinny little man with pince-nez glasses.

A BANK TELLER IN MINEOLA

A BANK OFFICIAL IN MINEOLA

SHERIFF PETE SMOOT : A typical Iowa small-town Sheriff.

BILLY : Smoot's young deputy, cold, intense and humorless.

BANK TELLER IN A SMALL TEXAS TOWN

AN ELDERLY GROCERY CLERK

A MASSIVE MUSCULAR BUTCHER

A POLICEMAN IN HOSPITAL

A SHORT-ORDER COOK

A HAMBURGER-STAND COUNTERMAN

AN OKIE FAMILY IN LOUISIANA

FARMER IN TEXAS : A 45-year-old man.

DAVIS : An old Negro sharecropper.

WOMAN WITH BABY AND CHILD : Texas farmer's family.

A FISHERMAN : With a string of catfish.

ALSO : POLICE, TOWNSPEOPLE AND OTHER INCIDEN-
TAL CHARACTERS IN TEXAS, MISSOURI, OKLA-
HOMA, KANSAS, IOWA, LOUISIANA.

BONNIE AND CLYDE

The film begins with a series of snapshots of the period against a black background. Interspersed with the photographs the credits appear in white type that dissolves into red.

At first the only sound that we hear is the clicking of a camera shutter, then, midway through the credits, as though coming from a great distance, we hear Rudy Vallee singing *Deep Night*.

After the final credit, two title cards, introducing the central characters, appear.

TITLE CARD 1 : *BONNIE PARKER, was born in Rowena, Texas, 1910, and then moved to West Dallas. In 1931 she worked in a café before beginning her career in crime.*

TITLE CARD 2 : *CLYDE BARROW, was born to a family of sharecroppers. As a young man he became a small-time thief and*

38

robbed a gas station. He served two years for armed robbery and was released on good behavior in 1931.

Dissolve to :

INTERIOR BEDROOM (DAY)

Extreme close-up of a woman's mouth. She is wearing bright red lipstick. The camera pulls back to reveal BONNIE PARKER. Blonde, somewhat fragile, intelligent in expression, she is standing in front of a mirror putting on make-up. She has overdone it in the style of the time : the rosebud mouth and so forth. As the film progresses her make-up will be refined until, at the end, there is none.

As the camera moves away, we see by degrees, that BONNIE is naked. Her nudity is never blatantly revealed to the audience, but implied. That is, she should be "covered" in various ways from the camera's point of view, but the audience must be aware of her exposure to CLYDE later in the scene. This is the only time in the film that she will ever be this exposed, in all senses of the word, to the audience. Her attitude and appraisal

CLYDE BARROW,
was born to a family
of sharecroppers. As a
young man he became
a small-time thief and
robbed a gas station.
He served two years
for armed robbery and
was released on good
behavior in 1931.

39

of herself here are touched with narcissism.

The bedroom itself is a second-storey bedroom in a lower-class frame house in West Dallas, Texas. The neighbourhood is low income. Though the room reveals its shabby surroundings, it also reveals an attempt by BONNIE to fix it up. Small and corny *objets d'art* are all over the tops of the bureaus, vanity tables, etc. (Little glass figurines and porcelain statuettes and the like.)

BONNIE finishes admiring herself. She walks from the mirror and moves slowly across the room, the camera moving with her, until she reaches the screened window on the opposite wall. The shade is up. There are no curtains. She looks out of the window, looking down, and the camera looks down with her.

EXTERIOR BEDROOM BONNIE'S POINT OF VIEW

Over her shoulder, we see the driveway leading to the garage, where there is an old black car parked, its windows open. We see a man walking up the driveway, somewhat furtively. He is a rather dapper fellow, dressed in a dark suit with a vest, a white collar, and a white panama hat. It is CLYDE BARROW. Obviously, he is about to steal the car. He looks it over, checking around him to make sure no passers-by are coming. He peers inside the front window to see if the keys are in the ignition. He studies the dashboard. BONNIE continues watching, silently. Finally she calls out.

BONNIE : *Hey, boy! What you doin' with my mamma's car?*

EXTERIOR DRIVEWAY

CLYDE startled, jumps and looks to see who has caught him. Obviously frightened, he looks up and his face freezes at what he sees.

EXTERIOR WINDOW CLYDE'S POINT OF VIEW

We now see what he is looking at : at the open window, revealed from the waist up, is the naked BONNIE. She looks down, an impudent half-smile on her face. She doesn't move or make any attempt to cover herself.

40

EXTERIOR CLOSE-UP

CLYDE's face changes from astonishment to an answering smile of impudence. (Seeing what he has, he realizes that this girl is clearly not going to scream for the police. Already they are in a little game instigated by BONNIE, sizing each other up, competing in a kind of playful arrogance. Before they speak, they have become co-conspirators).

BONNIE is still smiling. Finally she speaks:

BONNIE : *Wait there!*

INTERIOR BEDROOM

Running from the window, she flings open a closet and grabs a dress, and shoes. She slips on the shoes, and flings the dress on, running out the door as she does.

As she comes running down the narrow staircase she buttons up her dress.

EXTERIOR DRIVEWAY

She flies out of the door, slamming it behind her, runs off the porch and continues quickly into the driveway. Four feet away from CLYDE, she stops on a dime. They stand there, looking at each other, smiling the same challenge. For a few seconds, no one speaks, then :

BONNIE putting him on : *Ain't you ashamed? Tryin' to steal an old lady's automobile.*

CLYDE with the same put-on : *Oh come on, now, what you talkin' about? I been thinkin' about buyin' me one.*

BONNIE : *Bull. You ain't got money for dinner, let alone buyin' no car.*

CLYDE, still the battle of wits going on : *Well, Ma'am, I tell you somethin'. I got enough money for a Coca-Cola and since it don't look like you're gonna invite me inside ...*

BONNIE : *Ho, you'd steal the dining room table if I did.*

CLYDE moves from his spot : *Go into town with me? How'd that be?*

BONNIE is starting to walk onto the sidewalk.

BONNIE : *I'm goin' to work anyway.*

41

EXTERIOR STREET MOVING SHOT

It is a hot Texas afternoon, all white light and glare. As they walk the block to town in this scene, their manner of mutual impudence is still pervading.

CLYDE : *You're goin' to work, huh?*

BONNIE : *Yeah.*

CLYDE : *What kind of work you do?*

BONNIE : *None of your business.*

CLYDE pretending to give it serious thought : *I bet you're a . . . movie star! Huh? A lady mechanic?*

BONNIE : *No.*

CLYDE : *A maid?*

BONNIE really offended by that : *What d'you think I am?*

CLYDE right on the nose : *A waitress.*

> BONNIE is slightly startled by his accuracy, and anxious to get back, now that he is temporarily one-up.

BONNIE : *What . . . what line of work are you in? When you're not stealin' cars?*

CLYDE mysteriously : *Well uh, I tell you, I'm lookin' for suitable employment at the moment.*

BONNIE : *Oh, ho, yes, but what did you do before?*

CLYDE coolly, knowing its effect : *I was in State Prison.*

BONNIE : *State Prison?*

> She shows her surprise.

CLYDE : *Uh-huh.*

BONNIE herself again : *Well, I guess, uh, some little old lady wasn't so nice.*

CLYDE tough : *It was armed robbery.*

BONNIE sarcastically : *My, my, tsk, the things that turn up in the streets these days.*

EXTERIOR MAIN STREET

They are now on a small-town street of barber shops, cafés, groceries, etc. At the moment, it is deserted. They continue walking down the empty street, talking. CLYDE looks the place over.

CLYDE : *Hey, what do y'all do for a good time around here? Listen to the grass grow?*

BONNIE : *I guess you had a lot more fun up at State Prison.*

CLYDE laughs, enjoying her repartee. They continue walking. At a hydrant, CLYDE stops.

CLYDE showing off, but serious : *I tell you, see my right foot.*

He points at his right foot.

BONNIE : *Yeah.*

CLYDE : *I chopped two toes off that foot. With an axe.*

BONNIE shocked : *What? Why?*

CLYDE : *To get off work detail. You wanna see it?*

CLYDE goes and rests his foot on the fire hydrant.

BONNIE a lady of some sensitivity : *No! . . .* She bends down : then turning cute : *I . . . I surely don't intend to stand here in the middle of Main Street and look at your dirty feet.*

They continue walking in silence past a few stores, each planning what next to say.

BONNIE : *Boy, did you really do that?*

Dissolve to :

EXTERIOR GAS STATION

Gas station up the block. BONNIE and CLYDE are seen leaning against the soft drink chest, their profiles silhouetted by the bright sun. They are drinking cokes. As they begin to talk, the camera moves in closer to them. CLYDE takes off his hat and rubs the cold coke bottle across his forehead; there is a match stuck in the corner of his mouth. BONNIE watches him.

BONNIE : *What's it like?*

CLYDE : *What you mean, prison?*

BONNIE deliberately : *No, armed robbery.*

CLYDE thinks it a silly question : *It ain't like anything.*

BONNIE, thinking she's heard proof that he's a liar : *Hah! I knew you never robbed any place, you faker.*

CLYDE challenged : *Oh, yeah?*

He studies her, then makes up his mind to show her.

CLOSE-UP GUN

He reaches in his jacket and pulls out a gun. The camera moves into a close-up of the gun, glinting in the sunlight.

EXTERIOR STREET

The camera pulls back to show BONNIE looking at it with

fascination. The weapon has an immediate effect on her. She touches it in a manner almost sexual, full of repressed excitement.

BONNIE goading him: *Yeah . . . But you wouldn't have the gumption to use it.*

CLYDE plays with the match in his mouth, narrowing his eyes and looking about him.

CLYDE, picking up the challenge, proving himself: *All right. Tsk. You just wait right here and keep your eyes open.*

EXTERIOR LITTLE GROCERY STORE ACROSS THE STREET
The camera remains just beyond BONNIE's shoulder so that throughout the following scene we have BONNIE in the picture, looking at what we look at.

CLYDE goes into the little store. We remain outside with BONNIE watching. For a minute nothing happens. We can barely see what is going on in the store. Then CLYDE comes out, walking slowly. In one hand he holds the gun, in the other

a fistful of money. He gets halfway to BONNIE and smiles broadly at her, a smile of charm and personality. She smiles back. The moment is intense, as if a spark has jumped from one to the other. The relationship, which began the minute BONNIE spotted him in the driveway, has now really begun. CLYDE has shown his stuff and BONNIE is "turned on".

CLYDE quietly : *Look. Come on.*

Suddenly the old man who runs the grocery store comes running out into the street, completely dumbfounded. He stands there and says nothing, yet his mouth moves in silent protest. CLYDE points the gun above him and fires. It is the first loud noise in the film and comes as a shock. The old man terrified, runs back into the store as fast as he can. CLYDE quickly grabs BONNIE's hand. The camera swings with them as they turn and begin to run down the street. A few yards and the stores disappear entirely. The landscape turns into that arid, flat and unrelieved western plain that begins where the town ends.

EXTERIOR AT THE EDGE OF TOWN

A tan-coloured car is parked at the end of the deserted main street. As soon as they reach it, CLYDE motions and BONNIE gets in. CLYDE runs to the front, lifts up the hood and crosses the wires to make it start. As he stands back, BONNIE calls to him :

BONNIE : *Hey, what's your name, anyhow?*

CLYDE slams the hood : *Clyde Barrow.*

He runs over to the door, opens it, shoves her over, and starts up the engine. The entire sequence is played at an incredibly rapid pace.

BONNIE loudly, to make herself heard over the running motor : *Hi, I'm Bonnie Parker. Pleased to meet you.*

EXTERIOR ROAD

VROOM ! The car zooms off down the road, doing 90. The fast country breakdown music starts up on the sound track, going just as fast as the car.

INTERIOR CAR

The car, still speeding, further down the road. CLYDE is driving, BONNIE is all over him, biting his ear, ruffling his hair, running her hands all over him — in short, making passionate love to him while he drives. The thrill of the robbery and the escape has turned her on sexually.

EXTERIOR CAR ANOTHER ANGLE

The car starts to go crazy in a comical fashion, manifesting to the audience just what is happening to the driver controlling it.

INTERIOR CAR BONNIE AND CLYDE

BONNIE is still all over CLYDE, throwing herself at him.

EXTERIOR CAR

The car swerves all over the road, raising clouds of dust. Another car comes down the road the other way and CLYDE's car swerves so much as to make the other guy drive right off the road onto the dirt.

INTERIOR CAR BONNIE AND CLYDE

CLYDE is trying desperately to drive with BONNIE practically on his lap, hugging and kissing him.

EXTERIOR CAR BONNIE AND CLYDE

The car hairpins off the road onto a shoulder beneath some trees where it slows down and finally stops with a jolt.

INTERIOR CAR BONNIE AND CLYDE

BONNIE and CLYDE appear to be necking heavily now, punctuated by BONNIE's squeals of passion as she squirms and hops about like a flea, trying to get to CLYDE. With savage coquetry she tears into her clothes and his.

BONNIE muffled: *C'mon, honey, c'mon, boy . . . let's go . . . let's . . .*

CLYDE muffled: *Hey, hey, slow down, slow down. Take it easy, you got my . . . my hat . . . Hey! Cut it out. Hey, slow down.*

He shoves her rudely away, slamming her into the far car door. Suddenly it looks as if they've been fighting. Both

47

The Real Life Bonnie Parker

48

unbuttoned and unglued, they stare silently at one another, breathing heavily.

CLYDE jumps out of the car, clearly shaken. Despite the fact that he may have encountered this situation many times before, it's one that no twenty-one-year-old boy in 1932 is sophisticated enough to dismiss easily with bravado.

BONNIE remains seated in the car. She seems terribly vulnerable. She fumbles about for a cigarette, too confused to figure out what didn't happen. CLYDE turns back and reaches through the car window from the driver's side, lighting it for her. BONNIE casts CLYDE a fishy stare, then accepts the light.

CLYDE, trying to be casual, even insouciant: *All right now. Look here. I might as well tell you right off. I ain't much of a lover boy. That don't mean nothing personal about you. I mean* . . . His voice cracks. *I — I — I never saw no percentage in it. Ain't nothin' wrong with me . . . I don't like boys.*

He backs out and bangs his head on the roof of the car.

BONNIE doesn't know what she thinks, and CLYDE is trying to gauge her reaction — whether she feels rejected or repelled. In fact, it's both — along with a little latent fascination.

BONNIE, finally spitting out smoke: *Boy . . . Boy . . . Boy . . .*

CLYDE a little annoyed: *Boy, what?*

BONNIE: *Your advertising is just dandy. Folks'd just never guess you don't have a thing to sell.* A little afraid: *Y-you'd better take me home, now.*

CLYDE, getting back into the car: *Now you wait a minute. Wait a minute.*

BONNIE: *Now don't you touch me!*

She gets out of the car, leaving CLYDE draped across the front seat, reaching after her. He shoots out, head first, his hat falling on the ground.

CLYDE shouting: *All right, all right, if all you want's a stud service, you get on back to West Dallas and you stay there, rest of your life!*

This stops her. Now CLYDE pours it on, with an almost maniacal exuberance that becomes more controlled as he gets control of BONNIE.

CLYDE: *You're worth more'n that, a lot more'n that, and you know it, and that's why you come along with me. You could find*

49

a lover boy on every corner in town. It don't make a damn to them whether you're waiting on tables or picking cotton, but it does make a damn to me!

BONNIE turning, intrigued : *Why?*

CLYDE : *What do you mean, why? Because you're different, that's why. You know, you're like me. You want different things. You got something better than bein' a waitress.*

    BONNIE is hooked now.

CLYDE continuing : *You and me travellin' together, we could cut a path clean across this state, and Kansas and Missouri, and Oklahoma and everybody'd know about it. You listen to me, Miss Bonnie Parker. You listen to me. Now how you like to go walkin' in the dining room of the Adolphus Hotel in Dallas wearing a nice silk dress and having everybody waiting on you? Would you like that? Does that seem like a lot to ask?*

BONNIE sighing incredulously : *Whooo . . .*

CLYDE : *That ain't enough for you. You got a right to that.*

    He stops, having begun to woo her to something more intense than a casual, physical coupling.

BONNIE : *Now . . . Hey! Hey! W-w-when'd you figure all that up?*

CLYDE : *Minute I saw you.*

BONNIE questioningly : *Why?*

CLYDE intensely, with real honesty : *'Cause you may be the best damn girl in Texas.*

INTERIOR ROADSIDE CAFE BONNIE AND CLYDE

    BONNIE and CLYDE are seated in a booth in a cheap roadside café. CLYDE is talking. He is telling her about herself.

CLYDE : *You're born somewhere around East Texas.*

BONNIE : *Yeah.*

CLYDE : *Come from a big old family.*

BONNIE: *Yeah.*

    He loves doing this and he does it well. During their conversation, the more he envisions BONNIE's life, the more instinctively accurate he becomes. She grows more and more fascinated, like a child watching a mind reader.

CLYDE : *You went to school, of course, but you didn't take to it much 'cause you was a lot smarter than everybody else, so you up and quit one day. Now . . .* CLYDE is thinking, playing it for all it's

50

worth . . . *When you was sixteen . . . no, seventeen, there was a guy who worked in a — in a —*

Pull back taking in BONNIE, favoring CLYDE.

BONNIE : *Cement plant.*

CLYDE : *Right. Cement plant. And you liked him 'cause he thought you was just as nice as you could be. And you almost married that guy, but then . . . you thought, "No", you didn't think you would. So then you got your job in a café . . .* CLYDE is getting closer to home now, hitting them right in there . . . *And now you wake up every morning and you hate it. You just hate it. You get on down there, and you put on your white uniform . . .*

BONNIE enthralled : *Pink . . . it's pink.*

CLYDE : *Uh huh . . . and them truck drivers come in there to eat your greasy burgers and they kid you and you kid 'em back, but they're stupid and dumb, boys with their big old tattoos on 'em and you don't like it . . . And they ask you for dates and sometimes you go . . . but you mostly don't, because all they ever try to do is get in your pants whether you want 'em to or not . . . So you go on home and you sit in your room and you think, now when . . . and how . . . am I ever . . . gonna get away from this? . . . And now you know.*

BONNIE is half-mesmerized by his talk. A WAITRESS comes with their food. A cheap, gaudy dame, she has spit curls on each temple in the style of the time. CLYDE looks at her and at BONNIE, who also wears a spit curl. As soon as the WAITRESS leaves, he says :

CLYDE pointing at her hair : *Change that. I don't like it.*

Without a word of protest, BONNIE immediately reaches in her bag and takes out a mirror. She holds it up and with the other hand, brushes back the spit curl into her hair. She never wears her hair that way again. When she has pushed it back she looks at CLYDE for his approval. He nods his okay. She smiles, puts back her mirror and begins to eat her food. She's ravenously hungry and eats with total concentration on her plate. CLYDE doesn't touch his food, just watches BONNIE eat for a minute.

CLYDE : *Shiiii . . . you're a knockout.*

EXTERIOR ROADSIDE CAFE (DAY FOR DUSK)

CLYDE and BONNIE emerge from the café into the early evening. They move toward the car they have stolen. Just beyond sits a newer, convertible model. BONNIE, about to open the door of their car, is surprised to see CLYDE head toward the newer car.

BONNIE : *Hey, that ain't ours.*

CLYDE : *Sure it is.*

BONNIE : *Look, b-but w-we came in this one.*

CLYDE : *That don't mean we have to go home in it.*

BONNIE runs over to the new yellow convertible and gets in beside CLYDE. He turns the key and they pull away from the café. They drive off into the distance accompanied by country music.

INTERIOR ABANDONED FARM HOUSE (DAY)

Wide shot of the parlor living room. The room is bare. In the middle BONNIE is waking, having slept on a couple of car seats covered with an old piece of tattered blanket. There are windows behind her. She looks about bewildered.

BONNIE : *Clyde . . . Clyde.*

She starts to panic and runs to the window. CLYDE comes running up to the window outside.

BONNIE relieved : *Oh.*

CLYDE : *Hey, lady.*

BONNIE chagrined at her fear : *Where you been keeping yourself?*

CLYDE : *Oh, I slept out by the car.*

BONNIE : *Oh . . . These accommodations ain't particularly deluxe. Huh?*

CLYDE : *If they're after us, I want the first shot. Now you come on out here. We got some work to do.*

BONNIE moves to the door and comes out of the house onto the verandah.

EXTERIOR FARM HOUSE FRONT YARD

On the dilapidated picket fence, six old bottles have been placed. As BONNIE joins CLYDE he turns and fires six quick shots. The bottles shatter.

BONNIE : *Shewww. You're good.*

CLYDE : *I ain't good. I'm the best.*

BONNIE : *And modest . . .*

They move round to the side of the building where CLYDE points to an old tire hanging by a rope from a tree. He means that to be BONNIE's target. He hands her a gun.

CLYDE : *Now see that there, now: set her spinnin'. Now . . .*

BONNIE fires. She misses.

CLYDE : *No, set her spinnin'.*

BONNIE : *Oh.*

CLYDE : *It's all right, it's all right. C'mon now, try it again. And try and get . . . Now this time come down slow, slow. Now, all right.*

BONNIE fires again and hits the tire. They both yell and laugh with delight. She smiles and blows the smoke from the barrel in pride and self-mockery.

CLYDE : *Aw, how 'bout that? Now ain't you something? I tell you. Look I'm going to get you a Smith and Wesson, go in your hand easier. Okay?*

BONNIE : *Yeah.*

CLYDE : *Now I want you to try something now.*

As CLYDE is talking, a farmer appears around the corner of

the building.

FARMER : *Heighdo.*

CLYDE whirls at the sound. He grabs the gun from BONNIE, shields her, and aims at the FARMER.

FARMER frightened : *No sir . . . no sir. You all go right ahead.*

CLYDE watches him warily. The FARMER backs away, his hands raised. CLYDE and BONNIE start to move toward the FARMER. All three move around to the front of the building. At a distance we see an Oakie car loaded with belongings. A woman with a baby in arms sits in front. A smaller boy stands outside the car.

FARMER : *Used to be my place. But it's not any more. Bank took it . . . Yessir, they moved us off. Now it belongs to them.*

He points at the foreclosure sign. It reads : "PROPERTY OF MIDLOTHIAN CITIZENS BANK. TRESPASSERS WILL BE PROSECUTED."

BONNIE : *Why, that's a pitiful shame.*

CLYDE shakes his head sympathetically.

FARMER bitterly : *You're damned right, ma'am.*

He looks up to see an old NEGRO who has come from a distant shack and now stands near CLYDE's car.

FARMER, nodding towards the NEGRO: *Me and him put in the years here.*

CLYDE loads the empty gun. Both he and BONNIE look at the FARMER.

FARMER: *You all go right ahead. We just come by for a last look.* He stands a moment looking at the house and then turns toward his family in the car. CLYDE and BONNIE look after him. CLYDE spins and fires three fast shots into the foreclosure sign. The FARMER stops and turns, looking at CLYDE.

CLYDE offers the gun to the farmer. He looks at it, then accepts it. He slowly takes aim at the sign and fires. It pleases him. He looks at CLYDE and BONNIE who smile.

FARMER: *You all mind?*

BONNIE and CLYDE are puzzled.

FARMER: *Hey, Davis, c'mon over . . .*

The NEGRO moves toward them. Now BONNIE understands. DAVIS and the FARMER look toward the house. The FARMER fires again. This time at a window. Another shot shatters more glass. The FARMER and DAVIS grin appreciatively. He hands the gun to DAVIS and nods toward the house.

FARMER: *That's right . . . Go on.*

DAVIS slowly raises the gun and fires at another window. It shatters and they can't keep from laughing. The FARMER's SON stands by the truck, watching.

SON: *Look!*

The two men draw closer to BONNIE and CLYDE.

FARMER: *Much obliged.*

He extends his hand. CLYDE shakes it.

FARMER: *My name's Otis Harris, this here's Davis. We worked this place.*

CLYDE formally: *This here's Miss Bonnie Parker.*

DAVIS: *Glad to meet you.*

CLYDE: *How're you. I'm Clyde Barrow.*

FARMER: *Clyde.*

The FARMER turns and moves toward his people. DAVIS moves toward his shack. CLYDE and BONNIE in the background.

CLYDE continuing: *We rob banks.*

BONNIE turns quickly to look at CLYDE. He smiles and nods.

EXTERIOR/INTERIOR CAR (DAY)
BONNIE and CLYDE are driving down a long, country road. It
is the next day. BONNIE is driving, CLYDE beside her.
CLYDE : *Look, I don't want you to worry about nothing. This is
going to be the easiest thing in the world.* He laughs. *Your mama
could take this bank.*

CLYDE is playing it cool, knowing she is scared. He thinks
he's James Cagney.
CLYDE : *All right? You just be ready if I need you.*

BONNIE's hands are tense on the wheel. Her face shows how
nervous she is now that the time has come.

CLYDE's face begins to show the tension he feels. They drive
in silence.

EXTERIOR BUSINESS STREET OF A LITTLE TOWN
We are still in the car. BONNIE pulls over and stops by the
bank. CLYDE is frozen in his seat, blinking furiously. We can

57

see that, for all his talk, he is scared too.

BONNIE quietly : *What are you waitin' for?*

That gets him. CLYDE throws the door open and jumps, practically dives out the door.

INTERIOR BANK

Through the window of the bank, we can see CLYDE get out of the car. There is a sign on the window which reads : "FARMERS STATE BANK CAPITAL $70.000°°" Something is very screwy here. The bank is dark, the blinds are half-down over the panes in the door, the paint is peeling.

CLYDE approaches through the door, looking around furtively.

CLYDE yelling : *All right now . . .*

The place is deserted but for one TELLER who is half-asleep over his books. CLYDE approaches and thrusts the gun through the bars at him.

CLYDE with a swagger : *This is a stick-up! You just take it easy and nothin' will happen to you.*

TELLER looking up with no fear, his voice calm and conversational : *Heighdy.*

CLYDE nonplussed at this : *Gimme the money!*

TELLER : *What money, mister? There ain't no money here.*

CLYDE totally befuddled at the turn of events : *What you talking about? This here's a bank ain't it?*

They face each other through the bars.

TELLER : *Huh, well it was a bank, but we failed three weeks ago.*

The camera pans around the bank. We see that it is empty, dusty and shuttered.

CLYDE furious : *All right, now, you get on out here . . . C'mon out here!*

CLYDE in a rage, goes behind the partition, grabs the TELLER and pushes him ahead with the gun. CLYDE is fuming. He forces the TELLER out the front door.

CLYDE : *You git out there and tell my girl!*

EXTERIOR BANK

BONNIE is still in the car. She is terrified as she sees CLYDE and the TELLER coming at her. She doesn't understand what is happening.

CLYDE shoving the TELLER forward: *C'mon, c'mon, you tell her what you told me.*
TELLER acting like a man who has had his sleep interrupted by lunatics: *The bank's failed ... I'm sorry, ma'am.*
BONNIE's reaction is one of hysterical relief and appreciation of the humor of the situation. She laughs uproariously, she can't stop laughing. This makes CLYDE madder than ever. He shoves the TELLER out of the way.

INTERIOR CAR
Completely humiliated, CLYDE gets in the car, shoving BONNIE over. She is still laughing. He takes her place at the wheel and points his gun out the window.

INTERIOR CAR CLYDE AND BONNIE
ANGLE TO INCLUDE BANK WINDOW
On the bank window is lettered: "CAPITAL $70.000°°"
CLYDE aims and puts a bullet through each of the zeros. We see each shot through. Then the entire window hangs there for a second and suddenly crashes. On the soundtrack, BONNIE's hysterical laughter.

INTERIOR CAR
Inside the car, CLYDE is still shooting while BONNIE laughs hysterically. The TELLER flinches and shields his face from the flying glass as CLYDE starts the car and drives away.

EXTERIOR SPEEDING CAR
The car is speeding down an open road. A truck, which approaches in the opposite direction, swerves out of the way of the car as CLYDE hurls it round the truck at top speed, tires squealing.

INTERIOR CAR
BONNIE has still not fully recovered from her mirth, but is quietening down because she sees that CLYDE is really mad and can't be pushed too far.
CLYDE steaming: *We got $1.98 and you're laughing.*
She tries to stop. The country music starts up on the soundtrack.

EXTERIOR ROAD
The car is driving down an open road.

EXTERIOR STREET
The car pulls down another street of shops in another little hick town. It pulls to a stop in front of a grocery store.

INTERIOR GROCERY STORE
There is an old CLERK behind the counter. CLYDE stands facing the CLERK. He is holding a bag of groceries in one hand and with the other he is pointing his gun at the CLERK who silently gets the goods he wants.
CLYDE thinking if he has forgotten something: *Let's see now . . . a loaf of bread, a dozen eggs, quart of milk, four fried pies.*

INTERIOR CAR
BONNIE waits outside with the engine running. She sucks her fingers nervously.

INTERIOR GROCERY STORE

The CLERK reaches over the counter and puts the four fried pies into the bag. CLYDE smiles and looks up impishly.

CLYDE : *Come on now, you sure you ain't got no peach pies?*

The CLERK shakes his head.

CLYDE : *I don't believe you . . .*

Suddenly looming beside CLYDE is the BUTCHER — an enormous giant of a man — brandishing a meat cleaver. Camera looks up at this formidable sight as the cleaver comes crashing down, missing CLYDE and sticking in the wooden counter. He grabs CLYDE around the chest in a bear hug and actually lifts him off the ground. The struggle is in silence. CLYDE is terrified, fighting wildly to get free. Suddenly there is a terrific crash as the fighting men knock a pile of merchandise over.

At the sound of this crash, BONNIE, still in the car, looks up, startled.

The gun in CLYDE's hand is pinned, because the man has CLYDE's arm pinned to his thigh. CLYDE tries to raise the

61

barrel at an upward angle to shoot, finally he is able to do so. He fires. The bullet enters the BUTCHER's stomach. The BUTCHER screams but reacts like a wounded animal, more furious than ever. He still holds CLYDE in a fierce hug, staggering around the store, knocking into shelves and spilling cans. CLYDE is hysterical with fear. The BUTCHER falls to his knees, but still he doesn't release CLYDE. In a panic, CLYDE drags the man to the door, trying to get out.

EXTERIOR GROCERY STORE

BONNIE, worried by the noise and CLYDE's prolonged absence, has got out of the car. She sees CLYDE and the BUTCHER holding his legs. She is terrified. CLYDE drags him out on the street. The BUTCHER won't let go. In blind fury, he pistol-whips the BUTCHER's head with two terrific swipes. Finally the BUTCHER lets go. Hysterical, CLYDE jumps away and leaps out of the doorway toward the car on the other side.

CLYDE shouting: *Get the hell outta here!*

BONNIE gets back into the car and CLYDE jumps onto the running board, shouting frantically.

CLYDE : *Go ahead, go ahead! Come on, come on! I'm on!*

They drive off at top speed and CLYDE gets into the car.

INTERIOR CAR

CLYDE is shaken. He speaks haltingly, panting; trying to get control of himself.

CLYDE : *He tried to kill me . . . Why'd he try to kill me? I didn't want to hurt him. Try to get something to eat round here and some son-of-a-bitch comes up on you with a meat cleaver. I ain't against him. I ain't against him.*

EXTERIOR SPEEDING CAR

The car is speeding down an open road. Country music on the soundtrack.

Dissolve to :

EXTERIOR FILLING STATION (DIFFERENT DAY)

CLYDE stands by the hood of a black coupé. BONNIE remains seated in the car. CLYDE is covered with sweat and grease — clearly he has gotten in his licks on the engine without success. The garage attendant, C. W. MOSS, blows into the fuel lines of CLYDE's car, his cherubic cheeks puffed up. There is a distinctly flat sound. Neither CLYDE nor BONNIE seems impressed by the noise C.W. is making.

As C.W. screws back the fuel line he gestures to BONNIE to turn the engine over. It purrs beautifully. CLYDE is astonished.

CLYDE : *Now you just tell me what was wrong with that, boy.*

C.W., moving back to screw on the gas cap : *Dirt.*

C.W. now stands between CLYDE and BONNIE.

CLYDE : *Dirt?*

C.W. continuing : *Dirt in the fuel line . . . Just blowed it away.*

CLYDE still can't get over it.

C.W. belches. He is embarrassed before BONNIE.

C.W. : *'Scuse me, ma'am . . . Is there anythin' else I could do for you today?*

CLYDE looks across to BONNIE. BONNIE gets the message. CLYDE moves toward the office doorway in the background.

BONNIE : *My, you're a smart feller. You sure do know a lot about automobiles, don't you?*

C.W., he has no idea he's being toyed with : *Yeah, I guess I do.*

BONNIE : *Well, um would you know what kinda car this is?*

C.W. touching it : *This is a 4-cylinder Ford Coupé.*

BONNIE : *No.*

C.W. : *H'h. Sure it is.*

BONNIE : *This is a stolen 4-cylinder Ford Coupé.*

C.W. jerks his hand off it as if he touched a hot stove.

CLYDE getting in the conversation : *Hey, you ain't scared, are you? Huh?* TO BONNIE : *I believe he is. Well that's a pity now, we sure coulda used a smart boy like that, who knows such a great deal about automobiles.* Suddenly business-like, to C.W. : *Hey you a good driver boy?*

C.W. getting quite confused : *Yeah, reckon I am.*

CLYDE pretending to cool on him : *No, he's better off here . . .*

BONNIE : *What's your name, boy?*

C.W. : *C.W. Moss.*

BONNIE : *Well, I'm Miss Bonnie Parker and this here is Mr Clyde Barrow. We . . . rob . . . banks.*

C.W. reacts with wide eyes, exclaiming :

C.W. : *Shew! Ohhh!*

C.W. spins round, amazed. He shuffles about, hammering his fist on a post.

CLYDE swiftly, testing his mettle : *Hey now, there ain't nothing wrong with that, is there?*

C.W. nervously : *No. No.*

BONNIE with a put-on sigh : *Uh-uh, Clyde, he ain't the one . . . Let's go . . .*

CLYDE : *Wait . . . Hey, boy! . . . You think you got the guts for our line of work?*

C.W. affronted, in his dumb way : *What you talking about? I spent a year . . . I spent a year in reformatory.*

BONNIE : *A man with a record!*

CLYDE : *Well, I know you got the nerve to short-change old ladies a-coming in for gas. What I'm askin' you is have you got what it takes to pull bank jobs with us?*

BONNIE : *Mr. C.W. Moss?*

C.W. anxious to prove himself : *Sure, I do. I ain't afraid, if that's*

what you think.
CLYDE : *Prove it.*

> C.W. walks away from the car. Camera remains where it was. We see him walk inside the gas station office, open the cash drawer, close it, and come out. He emerges with a fistful of money. He walks over to BONNIE and drops the money on her lap. We see the bills flutter down. Not a word is spoken. CLYDE reaches back and opens the rumble seat.

CLYDE : *Yeah. Gonna be all right.*

> C.W. climbs in. The sound track picks up a hillbilly tune as they drive off down the road.

INTERIOR HOSPITAL ROOM

A small ward with a bed. On it, covered by a sheet which humps up like a mountain over his enormous stomach, is the BUTCHER. His head is propped up on a pillow and he sips a liquid through a bent glass straw. Camera is on the left side of the head of the bed, seeing the BUTCHER in a three-quarter profile. On the opposite side of the bed stands a uniformed

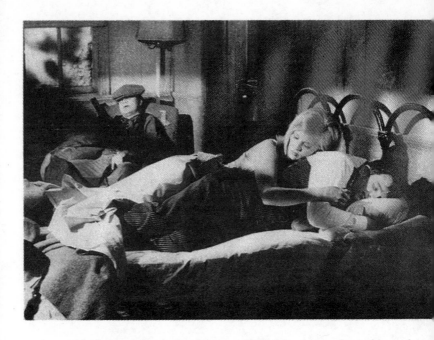

patrolman who is in the act of flashing mug-shot photos for the BUTCHER to identify his assailant. The lawman holds a stack of them in front of them, swiftly changing the cards like a grade-school teacher with her flash cards. At each picture, the BUTCHER grunts negatively, and goes on sipping from his glass straw. One picture, two, three go by. The fourth picture is a mug shot of CLYDE with the number 990830 printed on it. The BUTCHER's eyes flick up and down and we dissolve to:

EXTERIOR MOTEL (NIGHT)
A painted wooden sign, lit by one attached light, which reads: "SPUETT'S TOURIST COURT — REASONABLE RATES — VACANCY".

INTERIOR ROOM IN MOTEL
Camera is close on BONNIE. She is awake and restless. Off-screen comes the measured snoring that we will think comes from CLYDE. BONNIE raises up and kneels over CLYDE. She needs him. CLYDE seems to snore on. The camera moves a bit

and we see that it is C.W. who is asleep on the nearby sofa, snoring. BONNIE drops back on her pillow. We move in close on CLYDE. He is awake.

EXTERIOR SMALL KANSAS TOWN (DAY)
A black and red car is driving into a small Kansas town. It is Saturday afternoon, sunny. The streets are filled with people, cars and wagons. C.W. is driving, BONNIE is in front with him, CLYDE is in the back. C.W. looks scared to death at the idea of robbing a bank. The car pulls up beside a black saloon, double-parked. BONNIE and CLYDE get out and walk toward a bank on the corner.

INTERIOR BANK
Cut to the interior of the bank, where we see a TELLER talking to a CUSTOMER.
CUSTOMER: *I'm afraid we're overdrawn again this time, but I think maybe my husband's pay check . . .*
BONNIE and CLYDE have come in. They assume the classic

67

positions — she at the door where she can cover the bank, CLYDE nearby.

CLYDE in a very quiet voice : *This is a stick-up.*

No one takes any notice of him.

CLYDE louder : *This here's a stick-up.*

This time everyone in the bank hears it. The people gasp and pull back. Everyone raises their hands. CLYDE and BONNIE move forward, brandishing guns. BONNIE carries a paper sack. CLYDE motions her to go from cage to cage and get all of the money. BONNIE begins doing so, while CLYDE keeps his gun trained on everybody. Scared, a woman drops her bag.

CLYDE urgently : *Leave it, leave it there. Leave it there.*

We see BONNIE get the money from the first TELLER, the second TELLER, then . . .

EXTERIOR SMALL TOWN STREET

Close-up of C.W. who suddenly looks delighted to see a parking space. A convertible parked in a tight spot has just pulled out.

Immediately he methodically begins to back in. It's a tight spot, and he has to cut the wheel, pull forward, cut some more, pull back and so on. The scene, for the audience, should be nervous and funny.

INTERIOR BANK

Inside the bank, a TELLER is helping BONNIE fill the brown paper sack with bank notes.

CLYDE : *Come on, come on, everything. Get it up here . . .*

EXTERIOR CAR STREET

C.W. waits outside in the car, anxiously.

INTERIOR BANK

CLYDE covers the people in the bank as he and BONNIE back toward the door.

EXTERIOR STREET

They run out of the door and look for where the car was, but it isn't there.

BONNIE looking round urgently: *Clyde? Where's the car? . . . What'd he do!*

C.W. suddenly realises what a stupid thing he has done. He tries to shoot out of the parking spot, but he can't. He has to go through the business of backing up, cutting the wheel and all of it. The scene is one of pure pandemonium.

CLYDE sees where C.W. has parked the car.

CLYDE: *Over here!*

BONNIE and CLYDE run toward the car where C.W. is still trying to move out of the parking spot. They jump in.

INTERIOR CAR

CLYDE frantic: *What the hell you doing, parking the car?*

BONNIE: *Go! Go! Hurry.*

EXTERIOR CAR

C.W. gets out of the spot, scraping and ramming fenders in the process. The car disappears at high speed as the TELLER runs out shouting:

TELLER: *Stop that car! Stop that car!*

INTERIOR CAR

CLYDE yelling: *Up ahead, cut left! Left.*

Suddenly a face looms up at the window. It is the TELLER. He has leaped onto the running board. His screaming can barely be distinguished from all the noise. CLYDE fires through the window.

CLOSE-UP (SPECIAL EFFECTS)

The face of the man explodes in blood. Then he drops out of sight.

EXTERIOR CAR

The car shoots off down the road, doing ninety. Police are firing at the escaping car; BONNIE and CLYDE are shooting out the back window; C.W. is almost having a nervous breakdown at the wheel.

INTERIOR MOVIE HOUSE (SAME DAY)
WIDE ANGLE ACROSS AUDIENCE AT SCREEN

The opening musical sequence of *Gold Diggers of 1933* is on the screen. Ginger Rogers sings "We're in the Money".

TIGHT SHOT OF AUDIENCE

In the audience, BONNIE sits, watching the movie intently. In front of her and several seats away, C.W. slouches down in his seat morosely. In the row between them is CLYDE. He is nervous and keeps watching the door. CLYDE is in a rage. He shifts in his seat. We hear the music of the song on the soundtrack.

CLYDE in a furious whisper: *You ain't got a brain in your skull. On account of you, I killed a man. And now we're all gonna be wanted for murder and that's you, too, boy.*

He slaps the back of C.W.'s head. C.W. is close to tears.

SHOT FROM BEHIND CLYDE SHOOTING TOWARD SCREEN

CLYDE: *Dumb head. Stupid.*

C.W. turns to CLYDE. CLYDE grabs him by the shoulder.

CLYDE: *Do a dumb ass thing like that again, boy, I'm gonna kill you.*

ANGLE AT BONNIE

She has been absorbed in the movie; is now disturbed by the noise. She turns to CLYDE from her seat on the aisle.

BONNIE: *Ssshh! If you boys wanna talk, why don't you all go outside?*

She turns back to the screen, to the movie which she is obviously enjoying enormously. The actors' voices are heard on the soundtrack. CLYDE takes a last angry whack at C.W.

INTERIOR CHEAP MOTEL BATHROOM (DAY)

BONNIE stands at the sink fixing her make-up in a mirror. Her make-up has become more conservative. She sings "We're in the Money". She finishes fixing herself up and regards herself quizzically, tilting her head to look at herself at different angles. She is smoking a cigarette and really studying herself.

INTERIOR BEDROOM

Camera looks through into the connecting bedroom. CLYDE is sitting on the edge of the bed cleaning the guns and oiling them. He is quiet and preoccupied.

CLYDE: *Bonnie?* . . . BONNIE continues singing . . . *H-hey, honey.*

As BONNIE enters the bedroom, he looks up.

CLYDE quietly: *Honey, c'mon, I want to talk to you for just a minute . . . Sit down, huh?*

BONNIE sits, a little taken off balance by his serious manner. But she listens quietly.

CLYDE: *Look, this afternoon we killed a man and we were seen. Now so far nobody knows who you are but they know who I am . . . and they're going to be running after me and, anybody who's runnin' with me. And that's murder. Now it's gonna get rough.*

BONNIE nods. CLYDE continues speaking carefully and gently: *Now look, I can't get out, but right now you still can. I want you to say*

71

the word to me and I'm gonna put you on that bus back to your
mama. 'Cause you mean a lot to me, honey, and I just ain't gonna
make you run with me.

BONNIE, moved by his offer, has tears in her eyes.

BONNIE : *No.*

CLYDE : *Huh?*

BONNIE : *No.*

CLYDE : *Now look, I ain't a rich man. You could get a rich man*
if you tried.

BONNIE : *I don't want no rich man!*

CLYDE : *You ain't gonna have a minute's peace.*

BONNIE doesn't like him in this mood. She tries to josh him
out of it.

BONNIE : *Eh, you promise? . . .*

CLYDE is pleased and touched by her reaction. He puts his
hand tenderly on her cheeks. Then he moves over to where
BONNIE sits on the bed. They lie back and he kisses her.
The kiss moves toward real love making. They are on the bed
and push the guns aside. Some fall to the floor.

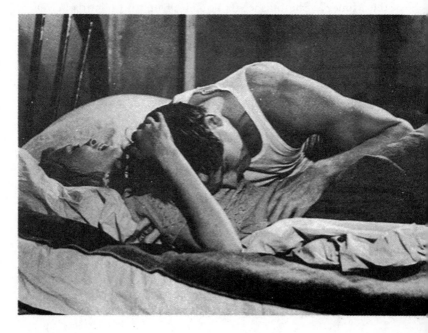

CLYDE breaks the embrace after it has reached a high pitch. He moves away from the bed toward the window. BONNIE remains on the bed looking at him. They are miserable.

CLYDE stands by the window, the light silhouettes him. He looks around the room, then starts to remove his shoes.

BONNIE turns to him from the bed. She smiles a comforting smile at him. She rolls over onto her back. Then sits up and looks back at CLYDE.

CLYDE comes over and lies beside her. They begin to make love. She kisses him passionately. Suddenly he breaks the embrace and moves away. BONNIE smiles bravely at him. She sits up and moves on top of him, caressing him and taking the initiative. CLYDE frowns anxiously as she begins to move down his body, caressing her way down his chest. He rolls away, burying his head in the pillow.

She looks at him. She is moved and pained for him. He pulls her toward him gently . . . She falls away from him. He moves away toward the window and rests his head on the pane.

CLYDE quietly: *Huh, least I ain't a liar . . . I told you I wasn't no lover boy.*

BONNIE tenderly: *Clyde.*

She smiles and shrugs her shoulders. Her look eases CLYDE and he almost smiles.

EXTERIOR CABIN FRONT OF THE MOTEL (DAY)

A car drives up to the cabin, honking the horn, wildly. The door of the cabin is open and CLYDE is standing beside another car outside. The car comes to a stop and BUCK BARROW jumps out. CLYDE leaps in the air, shouting:

CLYDE: *Buck! Buck!*

BUCK BARROW is a jovial, simple, big-hearted man. A little chubby, given to raucous jokes, knee-slapping and broad reactions. He is, in many ways, the emotional opposite of his brother. It doesn't take much to make him happy.

The brothers are overjoyed at seeing one another. They hug each other.

BUCK: *Clyde! You son-of-a-bitch.*

They laugh happily and begin sparring with each other, faking punches and blocking punches — an old childhood ritual.

74

There is a great feeling of warmth between the two brothers
CLYDE is more outgoing than we have ever seen him before.

CLYDE : *Buck! Hey! All right now . . . beat up at there, boy.*

BUCK : *C'mon on boy, hey! Hey! C'mon! C'mon, hey! C'mon boy
. . . you can do better than that! C'mon! Hey!*

CLYDE : *Hey, gee . . . Hey, hey, hey . . . How's mama?*

BUCK : *Oh, fine, fine. Sister — sister sent her best to you.*

CLYDE : *Filling out there, boy. Must be that prison food.*

BUCK : *No, no, no, it's . . . it's married life . . . and, you know what
they say, it's the face powder that gives a man interest, but . . .*

CLYDE : *Yeah?*

BUCK : *. . . but it's the baking powder that keeps him home! Huh?
Hey . . .*

CLYDE : *What?*

BUCK : *I want you to meet my wife, Blanche.* To BLANCHE : *This is
my baby brother.*

INTERIOR BUCK'S CAR
His wife, BLANCHE, sits in the passenger seat, clutching a movie

magazine.

BLANCHE BARROW, is the direct opposite of BONNIE. She is a house-frau, no more and no less, not terribly bright, not very ambitious, cuddly, simpering, madly in love with BUCK, and desirous of keeping their lives on the straight and narrow.

CLYDE shaking her hand: *Howdy-do. It's real nice to know you.*

BLANCHE: *How do you do.*

BUCK beams with pleasure, thinking they must like each other.

CLYDE: *Hey, Bonnie! Hey, hey, Bonnie!*

He drags BUCK over to the cabin. BONNIE comes out, standing on the steps. The screen door slams behind her.

BUCK bounds over to BONNIE, all jollity.

BUCK grabbing her: *Hi . . . Is it? Ooohhh boy! Ummm! Is this Bonnie?* CLYDE nods. *I hear you're takin' real good care of the baby of the family, huh? Hey! sis, I'm just so real glad to meet you!* He hugs her; BONNIE just lets herself be hugged. *Come over here.* Breaking the hug. *I want you to meet my wife, Blanche.* They go over to the car. BUCK to BLANCHE: *This here is Bonnie.*

BONNIE stiffly: *Uh, hi.*

BLANCHE stiffly: *Hello.*

There is an awkward pause. Suddenly the screen door opens and C.W. comes out, dressed in his underwear. BLANCHE can hardly stand it.

CLYDE: *Hey, everybody, this is C.W. Moss . . . My brother Buck and his wife, Blanche.*

C.W. friendly: *Howdy, everybody . . . Heighdy, y'all.*

BUCK sits on the running board. BONNIE is standing leaning on the hood while C.W. goes over to BLANCHE. With his characteristic one-track intensity, he decides to act just as friendly as he can with BLANCHE, ignoring the fact that he's standing there in his underwear. BLANCHE, however, is not ignoring it.

C.W.: *Howdy, Mrs. Barrow, or may I call you Blanche? Blanche? Hey, well I surely am pleased to meet you.* Shaking her hand; BLANCHE is slowly going crazy with mortification: *How did you find us here in this neck of the woods? Boy, you sure picked a good day for it. Oh, is that a new "Screenland Magazine"? Uh, is there any new pictures of Myrna Loy in there? 'Cause she's my favorite picture star.* Reaching forward to take the magazine: *Uh, may I?*

BLANCHE is starting to edge over to BUCK in sheer panic at this strange young man in his BVD's, but C.W. takes no notice of it. BLANCHE finally grabs BUCK. BONNIE watches it all, smirking.

BUCK : *Hey, there, lemme get the Kodak here!*

BUCK goes to his car and gets a folding Brownie camera.

BUCK : *We'll take some pictures.*

CLYDE lighting up a cigar : *Come on, put your pants on, boy. We're gonna take some pictures.*

C.W. goes into the cabin.

BUCK : *Come on, Blanche get . . . get out of there.*

CLYDE drags BLANCHE across to have her picture taken.

BLANCHE getting kittenish, and overdoing it : *I'm a mess. Been driving all day, honey. I'm a mess.*

BUCK : *Over there. Over there. Come on now.*

CLYDE : *Come on now.*

BONNIE watches BLANCHE'S behavior with hardly-veiled disgust.

BUCK : *Now hold onto her there.*

77

BLANCHE : *Wait a minute . . . Look out Buck!*

BUCK snaps the picture as BLANCHE is just about to move out of it.

BUCK pleased : *I got it.*

BLANCHE with unbecoming girlish outrage : *Did you take my picture, Buck? Well I declare.* She stamps her foot. *I asked you not to take my picture.*

CLYDE goes and gets a machine gun from the black saloon.

CLYDE : *Hey, Buck, get one of this.*

BUCK : *Hey, uh. Brother, I . . . want to talk to you later on.*

CLYDE giggles. He sits on the fender of the car and poses like a movie tough.

BUCK taking the picture : *Hold it.*

CLYDE still posing on the fender : *You got that.*

BUCK : *Yeah.*

CLYDE kisses the gun.

BUCK giving CLYDE the camera : *Hey, now, you, uh . . . you take one of me and my missus, here.*

CLYDE : *All right.*

BUCK puts his arm around BLANCHE.

BLANCHE : *Honey, I don't want to.*

BUCK : *Come on, Blanche!*

BLANCHE : *Honestly, I don't want a picture taken. I don't . . . Don't make me take it. Honey, I can't do it, Buck.*

CLYDE : *Oh, come on, Blanche. Come on.*

BUCK : *Come on over here. Come on. You look over there at the birdie anyhow.*

BUCK grasps BLANCHE in a bear hug.

BUCK : *Come on, give old Buckie . . .*

CLYDE looks up.

BUCK : *. . . a big kiss.*

CLYDE : *Be serious. Be serious.*

BUCK and BLANCHE are cheek to cheek, their arms round each other, posing and grinning in front of CLYDE's car.

CLYDE : *Hold . . . still.*

CLYDE takes the picture.

BLANCHE : *Oh, I don't know.*

CLYDE throwing her a challenge : *Hey, let me take one of Bonnie —alone. Come on, honey, huh?*

Bonnie grins at him and responds with amused arrogance.
Bonnie yanks the cigar from Clyde's mouth, smokes it and poses:
Okay.

Bonnie has taken up an arrogant pose, standing with one foot
on the front fender. She takes the gun out of her belt, points
it toward them, looking very tough. Then she leans sensually
against the radiator with one arm on a headlamp, drawing
back her jacket.

Clyde : *All right, now . . . Aw, honey.*

C.W. comes out from the house, dressed. He grins and jumps
up and down. Bonnie continues to pose solemnly.

Clyde coaxing : *Hey, come on now, a little smile. Don't you want
to smile, eh? Ready-y-y-y-y-y?*

Clyde snaps the picture. Everyone but Blanche laughs.

Buck, drawing Clyde aside : *Come on, I . . . want to have a chat
with you. Come on.*

Clyde handing C.W. the camera : *C.W., you take the girls'
picture.*

C.W. to Blanche : *Why don't you step in there with Bonnie?*

INTERIOR CABIN

BUCK and CLYDE come into cabin. Camera goes with them. The bedroom is dark, the shades pulled down. There is an aura of boys' club-house *camaraderie* in this scene.

CLYDE : *What did you think of her?*

BUCK : *Bonnie? She's a peach.*

BUCK shuts the door.

BUCK : *Hey,*

CLYDE : *U'huh?*

BUCK : *Uh, come on now, tell me true.*

CLYDE : *What?*

BUCK : *Is she as good as she looks?*

CLYDE acting up to the situation : *She's better.*

Suddenly BUCK becomes serious.

BUCK : *Hey, listen . . . It was . . . it was either you or him, wasn't it?*

CLYDE : *What?*

BUCK conspiratorally : *The guy that you killed. You had to do it, didn't you? Was either you or him?*

CLYDE : *Now, he put me on the spot. I had to. Right, I had to. Right . . . I had to.*

BUCK : *I . . . I . . . I knew you did.*

They are protecting each other, like two kids keeping a secret from Mom.

BUCK : *Don't say anything to Blanche about that.*

CLYDE : *All right . . . Hey, that time you broke out of jail. That true she, she talked you into going back?*

BUCK embarrassed : *Yeah, you hear about that? H'h.*

CLYDE : *H'h, that true?*

BUCK, it is obvious he had hoped CLYDE hadn't known about it : *Yeah, yeah.*

CLYDE : *Well, I won't say anything to Bonnie about it.*

BUCK : *I appreciate that.*

They look at each other, and laugh, somewhat embarrassed. There is now a long pause — a lull in the conversation, as if they asked each other all the questions and are now out of things to say. It is too much for BUCK, the natural enemy of silence, who suddenly claps his hands together and bursts out animatedly :

BUCK : *Whooaaa . . . who! We're going to have ourselves a time, boy.*

CLYDE matching his merriment : *Yeah, we surely are.*

BUCK : *Whoooooo!* A pause, then : *What we gonna do?*

CLYDE : *Well, how's this? I figured we all drive up in Missouri. They ain't lookin' for me up there. We find a nice little place to hole up in. We have us a regular vacation. All right?*

BUCK : *Yeah. Uh . . . No trouble now.*

CLYDE : *Ohhhh . . . I'm not lookin' to go back to prison.*

BUCK : *I heard in prison that you had a little trouble there. You was a-cuttin' up your toes.*

CLYDE : *You heard about that, eh? Yeah, well I did a little toe cutting.* Ironically : *That ain't but half of it. I did it so I could get off work detail. You know, breaking them damn rocks with a sledge hammer night and day.*

BUCK : *I know it.*

CLYDE : *And you know what? The very next week I got paroled. H'h! I walked out of that god-forsaken jail on crutches . . . Ain't life grand?*

EXTERIOR ROAD (DAY)
We see the two cars, one behind the other, driving down a main road.

INTERIOR FIRST CAR
CLYDE is driving, BUCK sits next to him. No one else is in the car.

BUCK : *Hey, you want to hear a story about this boy, he owned a dairy farm, see . . . And his old ma, she was kind of sick, you know. And the doctor, he called him over and said, "Listen, your ma, just lying there, she just so sick and she's weakly and I want you to try to persuade her to take a little brandy, see . . . just to pick her spirits up, you know." And, "Ma's a teetotaler," he says, "she wouldn't touch a drop." "Well, I'll tell you what to do." That's the doc. "Now I tell you what to do, you bring in a fresh quart of milk every day and you put some brandy in it, see. And you try that." So, so he did, and he . . . he doctored it all up with the brandy—fresh milk—and he gave it to his mama, and she drank a little bit of it. She didn't . . . know. So next day he brought it in again, and she drank a little more ; you know. And so the . . . it*

81

went on that way for the third day, just a little more, and the fourth day she was—you know, took a little more . . . and then finally a—one week later, uh, he gave her the milk, and she just drank it down, boy, she swallowed the whole, the whole thing, you know, and she called him over and she said, "Son, whatever you do, don't sell that cow!"

They both explode in laughter.

BUCK : *"Don't sell the cow."*

INTERIOR SECOND CAR

At the top of the laugh, cut to the interior of the second car, riding right in back of them. The atmosphere is completely unlike the cozy and jolly scene preceding. We have dead silence. BONNIE is driving, smoking a cigarette, grim. BLANCHE —seated as far away as she can get from BONNIE without falling out of the car—makes a face at the cigarette smoke, rolls down the window for air. C.W. is in the back seat, just staring.

EXTERIOR GARAGE APARTMENT

A residential street in Joplin, Missouri, showing a garage apartment above a double garage. Camera sees BUCK talking to a dapper gent with keys in his hand. BUCK pays him. The man tips his hat and gets into his car which is parked outside one of the garages.

LANDLORD : *All right, you got the keys now, haven't you?*

BUCK : *I got them.*

LANDLORD : *Fine.*

BUCK : *We'll be seeing you. Bye bye.*

LANDLORD : *Bye, Buck.*

BUCK gestures to CLYDE who drives BUCK's car into the driveway. BONNIE follows, driving CLYDE's car with BLANCHE beside her. CLYDE stops beside BUCK, who leans into the car, and says :

BUCK : *I give him a month's rent in advance. We're all set. Let's get inside.*

BUCK jumps onto the running board of the other car.

BUCK : *Honey-lamb. I'm taking you to our first home.*

BLANCHE giggles. The two cars pull up before the garage and the people start to descend.

INTERIOR GARAGE APARTMENT

A winded BUCK enters and puts down BLANCHE. As others behind him carry in their things and disperse throughout the apartment.

BUCK : *"Here comes the bride." What d'you think honey?*

BLANCHE : *Ohhh. Just perfect.*

BUCK : *This is your first home.*

BLANCHE : *Isn't this lovely?*

BUCK goes over to the telephone.

BUCK : *He give me the grocery number.*

BLANCHE : *Oh, it's perfect for all of us, isn't it . . . Buck?*

BUCK : *4-3-3-7, please . . . Hi, there, Speedie's Groceries? I want to order up a mess of groceries. Ah . . . 443 Hilldale Avenue. Hilldale Avenue.*

BLANCHE : *Oh look, it's so clean, Buck. And a Frigidaire, not an icebox!*

She opens the refrigerator door and finds old rotting food. Hastily she closes the door.

BUCK : *Oh, about 8 pounds of porkchops, 4 pounds of red beans,*

*some, uh, Chase and Sandborn coffee, uh, about, uh, eight bottles
of Dr. Pepper . . .*

BLANCHE : *Hey darling, ain't that clever?*

INTERIOR LIVING ROOM

Open on BONNIE and CLYDE. He is cleaning guns. She is
watching something off-screen. We hear a clicking sound.
As the clicking sound increases we cut to see that BUCK and
C.W. are playing checkers. CLYDE is leaning over C.W.'s
shoulder. BUCK has just beaten him. All three yell with
laughter. CLYDE, who has been watching BONNIE, smiles at
her. BLANCHE whoops. BUCK starts to set up the game again.

BLANCHE ruffles his hair : *You sure can play checkers . . . You need
a haircut. You're looking just like a hillbilly boy.*

A look of disgust crosses BONNIE'S face.

BLANCHE off-screen : *You are just like an old man. Playing checkers
all . . . the time, don't pay any attention to your poor little old
meek wife.*

BUCK off-screen : *Boy, you're never gonna beat me, but you just
keep tryin', you hear?*

C.W. off-screen : *Come on, I'm going to whip you all over
Louisiana.*

BONNIE is standing by the bedroom door. Slowly, a wicked
little smile edges across her face. She watches for a moment
more, then with the most ingenuous look she can muster up,
she beckons to CLYDE to follow her into the bedroom. A little
puzzled, CLYDE follows.

INTERIOR BEDROOM

BONNIE closes the door and immediately begins fussing with
CLYDE's hair, doing a scathing imitation of BLANCHE. Though
her miming expresses her irritation at being closeted with the
Barrow menage, it is also a peach doing an imitation of a
lemon.

BONNIE doing an unmerciful imitation : *Daddy, you sure do need
a haircut . . .* She ruffles his hair *. . . Why, you look like a little
old hillbilly, I do declare.*

CLYDE forces her down on the bed.

CLYDE amused but cautionary : *Don't talk that way . . . when she's right there in the next room.*

BONNIE with a mock-pout, but with an edge to it : *There is always somebody in the next room, in this room or in ever' other kind of room.*

Suddenly, BONNIE straightens up to a kneeling position, and cocks her head. When she speaks now it is with a simple plaintiveness.

BONNIE : *Why honey, don't you ever just want to be alone with me?*

CLYDE looks up to BONNIE, affectionately.

CLYDE : *Well, I always feel like we're alone.*

BONNIE, it's terribly important to her : *Do you, baby?*

CLYDE getting up : *I'm hungry . . . Hey, Buck!*

CLYDE leaves. BONNIE, alone, looks up in alarm as the doorbell rings.

EXTERIOR GARAGE APARTMENT
A DELIVERY BOY is there with two big sacks of groceries. He

85

rings. A moment later BONNIE appears at the front door window.

DELIVERY BOY: *Groceries M'am.*

She unlocks the door and comes out.

BONNIE: *How much?*

DELIVERY BOY: *Six dollars and forty-three cents.*

BONNIE: *Forty-three?*

DELIVERY BOY: *Yes M'am.*

BONNIE says "All right," pays him and goes to take the bags from him.

DELIVERY BOY: *Thank you. Here M'am, let me help you with . . . those bags are heavy.*

BONNIE curtly: *No thanks, I'll get them.*

DELIVERY BOY: *Okay, M'am.*

She takes the heavy bags and hefts them up and turns and walks up the stairs. They are obviously very heavy for her. The DELIVERY BOY looks puzzled at this behavior.

BONNIE, nodding toward the door: *Uh, just get the door.*

DELIVERY BOY: *Okay.*

As BONNIE reaches the top steps, voices are heard.

BLANCHE'S VOICE: *Clyde, look at Bonnie.*

CLYDE'S VOICE: *Get down. Close the door.*

CLOSE-UP THE DELIVERY BOY

A look of suspicion comes across his face.

Dissolve to:

INTERIOR GARAGE APARTMENT

BONNIE seated in the living room. The others grouped around her.

BONNIE reading from a pad; in a recital voice: *It's called "The Ballad of Suicide Sal."* She pauses for effect; then begins:

"We each of us have a good alibi
For being down here in the 'joint';
But few of them really are justified
If you get right down to the point.
You've heard of a woman's glory
Being spent on a downright cur."

BUCK interrupting: *Did you write all that yourself?*
BONNIE: *Do you want to hear this . . . or not?*
    As she reads, the camera moves around the room picking out everyone's reaction. CLYDE is looking and listening seriously. BUCK is grinning. C.W. is blank. BLANCHE is about to start cooking in the kitchen.
BONNIE: *"Still you can't always judge the story*
       As true, being told by her.
       Now 'Sal' was a gal of rare beauty,
       Though her features were coarse and tough—"
BUCK: *I knew that old girl. She was cockeyed and she had a hare-lip and no teeth!*
    BONNIE flashes him a look that could kill. C.W. laughs at BUCK's words.
CLYDE annoyed: *Hey, Buck, come on now . . . Go ahead.*
BONNIE continues: *"Now 'Sal' was a gal of rare beauty,*
       Though her features were course and tough;
       She never once faltered from duty
       To play on the 'up and up'.
       Sal told me this tale on the evening
       Before she was turned out free."
    Still listening, CLYDE gets up from his chair and walks slowly over to the living room windows. The camera angled slightly above him, sees down the street. We see two police cars quietly pulling up. One of them parks in the driveway to block escape from the garage, the other stays on the street. CLYDE turns and looks out of the window.
BONNIE off-screen: *"And I'll do my best to relate it*
       Just as she told it to me—"
CLYDE moving away from the window: *Hey, hey! The law's outside!*
BONNIE: *What!*
CLYDE: *They're blocking the driveway!*
    NOTE: The three major gun battles in this film, of which this is the first, each have a different emotional and cinematic quality. The quality for this Joplin debacle is chaos, hysteria, extremely rapid movement and lots of noise. The audience should be assaulted. From the moment CLYDE cries out, and throughout all the following action, BLANCHE, in blind panic,

87

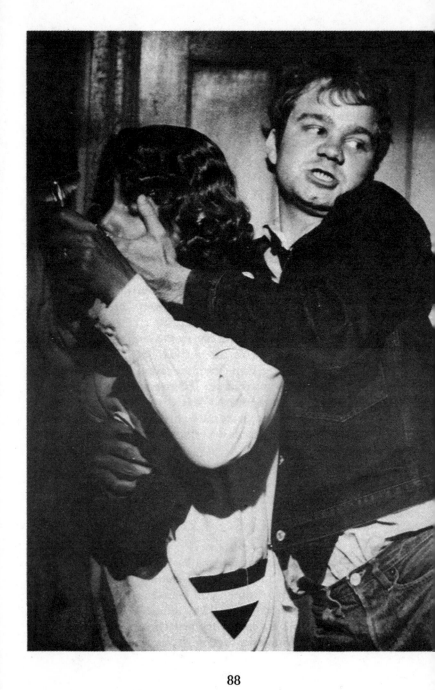

drops the frying pan and screams hysterically. The scream persists through the gunfire, never lessening on the soundtrack. Its effect should be at first funny to the audience, then annoying, and finally terrifying.

C.W. grabs her and pushes her over toward the door. Camera cuts back to the living room. Everyone else leaps into action. Guns begin blazing from everywhere; we rarely see who is shooting at whom.

EXTERIOR GARAGE APARTMENT
The police, we see in outside shot, are lined up in the street, firing. There are about ten of them.

INTERIOR GARAGE APARTMENT
Window panes shatter. The gang fire. BLANCHE comes up to BUCK, hysterical.

BLANCHE screaming: *Buck, Daddy! Please get us out of here!*
BUCK angrily: *Shut up!*

EXTERIOR GARAGE APARTMENT
Two policemen fire from behind an out-house . . .

INTERIOR GARAGE APARTMENT
. . . shattering a lamp on the dressing table. C.W. reloads his
gun. BONNIE and CLYDE are firing from the living room
window. BUCK is reloading guns and passing them to CLYDE.
BUCK : *They got us blocked! We got to get the car out!*
BUCK rushes through the apartment with a shotgun, followed
by BLANCHE, shouting :
BUCK : *Cover me!*

EXTERIOR GARAGE APARTMENT
BUCK, crouching, shooting with one hand, comes up to the
garage, followed by BLANCHE. A cop fires. BUCK fires back and
the cop falls dead in the street. BUCK, firing, dashes to the
police car blocking their escape and releases the hand brake.
BLANCHE, however, in utter panic, just runs right out of the
front door, and begins running down the quiet residential

street, going nowhere, anywhere.

At that moment the gang's car crashes through the garage door. BONNIE, CLYDE and C.W. are all inside, still shooting madly. BUCK leaps on the running board.

Two policemen fall dead or wounded. Another one is hurled through a fence by the blast of a shot gun.

BUCK jumps inside the car with the others. The gang's car rams the police car, sending it down the driveway and into the police barricade.

The gang's car turns into the street and zooms off in a hail of bullets.

POLICEMAN'S VOICE: *Keep firing, keep firing! Damn you! Load and fire! Damn you.*

Inside the car, BUCK leans forward.

BUCK: *Where's Blanche? Where's Blanche?*

BLANCHE is running wildly down the street. The car pulls up alongside her; the back door is flung open and, in almost the exaggerated style of an animated cartoon, two hands reach out, lift BLANCHE off her feet and pull her into the car. They speed away.

INTERIOR CAR

The inside of the car, still speeding. The gang is not being pursued now, but CLYDE is driving at 90. BLANCHE is moaning and crying. BONNIE, in front, turns around furiously.

BONNIE: *Dammit! You almost got us killed!*

BLANCHE screaming and crying at the same time: *What did I do wrong? I thought you'd be happy if I got shot!*

BONNIE screaming: *Yeah! Yeah! It would have saved us all a lot of trouble!*

BLANCHE: *Buck, don't let that woman talk to me like that!*

BUCK is caught in the middle of a bad situation, knowing BLANCHE is wrong, but trying to soothe her.

BUCK: *You shouldn't have done that, Blanche.* Quietly: *It was a dumb thing to do.*

BLANCHE, switching tactics: *Oh, Buck, please. I didn't marry you to see you get shot at . . . Please, let's go—let's leave . . . Let's get out of here and leave. Tell him to please stop the car and let us out.*

BUCK grabbing her: *I can't. I killed a guy. Now we're all in this.*

91

BLANCHE : *Please!*
> BLANCHE becomes hysterical again. BONNIE turns round exploding :

BONNIE : *Will you shut up! Just shut your big mouth! At least do that much, please, just shut up!*
CLYDE shouting : *Cut it out, Bonnie!*
> BONNIE is affronted. BLANCHE continues sobbing.

BONNIE curtly : *Stop the car. I want to talk to you.*
> Without a word, CLYDE stops the car.

EXTERIOR ROADSIDE
> CLYDE drives the car off the road onto the verge, tires screaming. He and BONNIE get out and walk fifteen feet away from the car. Both are irritated and touchy. Camera follows them.

BONNIE : *Get rid of her.*
CLYDE : *I can't get . . . She's Buck's wife!*
BONNIE snapping her words : *Well, then, get rid of them both.*
CLYDE : *Why? What's the matter with you anyway?*
BONNIE : *She's what's the matter with me.* She starts to cry . . . *She —she's nothing but a dumb, stupid back country hick . . .*
CLYDE angrily : *Now, you look . . .*
BONNIE : *She ain't got a brain in her head.*
CLYDE, really pissed-off at BONNIE : *What makes you any better? What makes you so damn special? You was just a West Dallas waitress. Spent half your time pickin' up truck drivers!*
> This hits home with BONNIE. He has said the unforgivable.

BONNIE raising her voice : *Stop it! Oh, big Clyde Barrow, you're just like your brother . . . ignorant, uneducated, hillbilly.* With deadly archness : *Listen the only special thing about you is your peculiar ideas about love makin'—which is no love makin' at all.*
> CLYDE stiffens. The two of them stand silent and tense, almost quivering with anger. They have stripped each other raw. CLYDE turns and looks back at the car. Everyone is waiting, watching them.
> BONNIE looks at CLYDE and her eyes reflect the realization of the pain she has inflicted on him. She softens.

BONNIE : *No-o! Oh, Clyde please, I didn't mean that. Listen, it, it was just all, all that shooting . . .* She leans toward him . . . *and*

all those guns. I got so scared. Please, honey, I didn't mean it.
They stand looking at each other. CLYDE raises his hands and places them round BONNIE's face, looking into her eyes—then he turns and begins walking back to the car. BONNIE walks alongside him. On the few steps back, she regains all her dignity and acts aloof from the others waiting for her. She reaches the car. CLYDE opens the door for her and she gets in like a great lady. He walks around to his side, gets in, and they drive off.

EXTERIOR ROAD (DAY)
Wide shot of a car—a different model from the preceding sequence—driving down a dirt back country road, mid-afternoon. It pulls up alongside an R.F.D. mailbox at the side of the road. A newspaper is sticking out of it. CLYDE reaches out, grabs the newspaper and drives on.

INTERIOR CLYDE'S CAR
BUCK is reading from the newspaper.
BUCK jubilantly: *"Law enforcement officers throughout the South-west are frankly . . .* He laughs *. . . amazed at the way in which the will-o'-the-wisp bandit Clyde Barrow and his yellow-haired com-panion, Bonnie Parker, continue to elude their would-be captors. Since engaging in a police battle, on the streets of Joplin, Missouri and slaying three of their number . . ."*
We notice CLYDE is wincing.
BUCK: *"Well . . . the Barrow gang has been reported as far West as White City, New Mexico, and as far north as Chicago. They have been credited with robbing the Mesquito Bank in the afore-mentioned White City, and the J.J. Landry Oil Refinery in Arp, Texas"* . . .
BONNIE: *Arp?*
Everybody laughs.
BUCK continues: *"The Sanger City National Bank in Sanger, Indiana, and the Lancaster Bank in Denton, Texas on three dif-ferent occasions. In addition to these robberies, the fast travelling Barrows have been rumored to have had a hand in the robbing of two Piggly Wiggly stores in Texas, and one A&P store in Missouri, though Chief Percy Hammond, who first identified Clyde Barrow's*

brother Buck . . .
BLANCHE : *Oh Lord!*
BUCK continues : *". . . as a member of the gang, expressed some doubt that these last robberies were committed by the Barrow Gang alone."*
C.W. : *Hey, Clyde, we ain't gonna see another toilet for another thirty miles. Why don't you pull up over here.*
CLYDE looks relieved.

EXTERIOR WOODED AREA
He pulls the car to a stop, gets out and goes off into the woods. We watch him vanish behind the trees.

INTERIOR CAR
BUCK is still scanning the newspaper.
BUCK : *Hey now, here's something! "Lone Cop Arrests Two Officers In Hunt For Barrows. Police Officer Howard Anderson's heart turned faster than his motorcycle when he forced to the side of the road a roaring black V-8 sedan in which were three men and a blonde-headed woman yesterday afternoon."*
Everybody laughs. BUCK continues to read, his voice remaining on the soundtrack.

EXTERIOR CAR
The camera is some distance away from the Barrow automobile and we see a car pull quietly to a stop in the foreground. A Texas Ranger, the only occupant, gets out. He is tall, big, a bit overweight, and sports a small handle-bar moustache. He draws his gun and slowly approaches the Barrow car from the rear. On the soundtrack BUCK's voice continues, as we see all this taking place.

INTERIOR CAR
C.W. and BONNIE are both listening attentively as BUCK reads.
BUCK : *". . . When he saw several machine guns in the car he was certain he'd caught Clyde Barrow, Bonnie Parker, and maybe Buck Barrow and the third un-identified member of the gang. It took a lot of telephoning and explaining to convince the motor-cycle cop that his captives were two highway patrolmen and a*

blonde-haired stenographer from the Highway Patrol." Haw!
Haw!

Everybody busts up with laughter.

EXTERIOR CAR

In the meantime, on screen, the Texas Ranger is slowly
approaching the back of the car. Suddenly CLYDE comes out
of the woods, *behind* the Texas Ranger. His gun is tucked in
his pants. In a second, he sees what is happening. BUCK'S voice
is continuing:

BUCK : *"Anderson was held up as an example for every other Texas
peace officer today. 'That was a mighty brave thing' explained
Highway Patrol Chief L. C. Winston."*

CLYDE whips out his gun. The following scene is played
exactly like a classic fast-draw in an heroic Western.

CLYDE : *Sheriff!*

HAMER, the Texas Ranger, spins around. Both men fire
instantaneously, but CLYDE has the draw on him, and the aim.
The gun goes flying from the sheriff's hand. A really razzle-
dazzle display of grandstand marksmanship from CLYDE.
Immediately the gang leaps from the car and surrounds the
Texas Ranger, guns drawn.

BUCK : *I never seen such shootin'!*

The gang grabs the man and takes his handcuffs from his belt.

CLYDE : *All right, all right.*

BUCK : *Get your hands up.*

CLYDE : *All right . . . Now you just get right over to that car.*

CLYDE makes him lean on the car's trunk, arms extended,
legs spread, while he frisks him. In general, everyone is
excited over the capture. BONNIE takes the sheriff's gun.

CLYDE examining the man's wallet, really surprised : *Well, now,
look here. We're in the custody of Cap'n Frank Hamer, and, er,
Frank here is a Texas Ranger.*

C.W. : *Sure 'nough, he is.*

REVERSE ANGLE ACROSS TRUNK

HAMER'S face, not visible to CLYDE or anyone else behind him,
is in the foreground. His gnarled, powerful hands tremble
slightly on the trunk, as though they might crinkle the metal

95

like so much tissue paper. His eyes stare toward camera relentlessly, unblinkingly, but without passion. They are shark's eyes. They have witnessed much carnage, devoured it, and are still wide open for more.

Throughout his capture he will remain totally impassive, hardly deigning to acknowledge the mere existence of the Barrow Gang. HAMER is tall and strong with a frightening face, a face that can impart evil. He is a man tightly under his own control. He holds on to whatever rages inside him. He is very aware of his position, professional and egoistic.

In the position he now finds himself, another set of factors are revealed by HAMER's personality, and they must be revealed solely by his lack of expression, his flat, emotionless quality and his eyes—that is, his utter contempt for criminals. He does not even deal with them—they are so beneath him that he conceives of only killing them, exterminating them.

BUCK : *Say there, peacemaker, I believe you got your spurs all tangled up there, haven't you? You're in Missouri, d'you know that, friend, huh?*

CLYDE has been going through the man's credentials. Not so pleasantly :

CLYDE : *D'you know you're in Missouri?*

C.W. : *He's lost, this Texas Ranger.*

CLYDE claps HAMER's hands behind his back, handcuffs him, and spins him around.

CLYDE, a little pissed : *Huh! I don't think he's lost. Them banks been offerin' extra reward money for us, and I think Frank just figured on some easy pickin's . . . Didn't you, Frank? . . . You know, Texas Ranger . . . You ain't hardly doing your job. You oughta be home protecting the rights of poor folk, not out chasing after us.*

HAMER flinches involuntarily. BUCK suddenly grows wary at CLYDE's mood. CLYDE leans toward HAMER. Suddenly, he lifts HAMER's huge bulk onto the fender, furiously knocking off his hat. BUCK intervenes.

BUCK trying to be casual : *Clyde, now hold on there. Take it easy there, Clyde. Oh watch it there, Clyde. Hold it there, Clyde! Clyde!*

CLYDE : *Look at that! Look . . . protecting the poor folks.*

BUCK : *Why do you want to take it so personal for?*

CLYDE: *Well, all right, we, we gotta discourage this here* bounty *hunting for the Barrow Gang.*

> BLANCHE looks *very* uncomfortable. She starts to say something, but BUCK intervenes.

BUCK: *What? What do you want to do with him then, huh?*

> A tense moment. CLYDE can't think of anything right away.

C.W. trying to be helpful: *Shoot him?*

BLANCHE gasps: *No!*

CLYDE: *Come on now, huh.*

C.W. trying again: *Hang him?*

BUCK amazed: *Hang him?*

REACTION BONNIE

> She shoots them an angry glance—this sort of thing is just what the gang doesn't want. She carefully gauges the moment to intervene.

BONNIE suddenly: *Uh-uh. Take his picture.*

CLYDE: *Huh?*

> CLYDE's not sure he's heard right. Neither is C.W.

BONNIE: *Mm!*

C.W.: *Take his picture?*

BONNIE pointedly ignoring C.W.: *We'll send it to all the newspapers. And then everybody's gonna see Captain Frank Hamer of the Texas Rangers with the Barrow gang* . . . moving demurely to HAMER . . . *And all of us just as friendly as pie.*

> They begin to grasp the possibilities.

BONNIE, continuing right on, coyly picking up HAMER's gun from the grill: *Now you know we are just about the friendliest folks you'd ever want to meet. Big old Texas Ranger waves his gun at us, and we just welcome him like he's one of our own.*

> BONNIE has her arm round HAMER's neck and she coyly strokes his moustache with the barrel of the gun.

CLYDE grinning widely: *Hey, Buck. Get the Kodak!*

BUCK relieved and excited: *Yeah* . . . *Hot dawggie.*

> HAMER is obviously not pleased with this turn of events. A sense of mounting glee at the kind of vengeance they are going to exact.

NEW ANGLE

Buck is fiddling with the camera, setting up the shot.

Buck: *Get him up there . . . On the . . . spare tire, Clyde.*

Clyde hoists Hamer bodily up onto the spare tire and then climbs up onto the back fender beside him. Bonnie tucks Hamer's gun into her belt.

Clyde: *All right, here we go, my friend. Now see what comes o' your mischief . . . not doing your job? You know, down in Duncanville last year . . .* Fixing the Texas Ranger badge back on his shirt *. . . poor farmers kept you laws away from us with shotguns. Now you supposed to be protecting them from us and they're protecting us from you. That don't make sense, do it?*

Bonnie is wearing the Texas Ranger's hat. She poses in pin-up girl style, one hand on her hip. Blanche looks on sullenly.

Buck: *You and . . . Bonnie first. Now you get right in there . . .*

Clyde grandly puts an arm on Hamer's shoulder, Bonnie looking up admiringly from the other side.

Buck: *When his Texas Ranger friends see this, he gonna wish he was . . . dead.*

Clyde: *Well, I'm mighty proud to have a Texas Ranger in the*

family.

BUCK: *Hold it, hold it!*

    BUCK takes the picture.

    BONNIE immediately hops onto the spare tire, next to HAMER.

BONNIE: *How's this?*

    She coyly loosens his tie, tousles his hair, and plants a big kiss on him while still ogling the camera. His attitude toward women is something that must be imparted without words. He regards women as secondary creatures of no importance. His attitude toward BONNIE, then, combines all of these feelings, for she is to him the very bottom of humanity—a criminal woman. BONNIE senses his contempt in a way that none of the others do. Her one desire is to crack his façade, to make him lose his cool, to force him to come to equal terms with her and then destroy him.

BUCK: *Oh, good, good! . . . I'm gettin' it, I'm gettin' it. Eh, wait, hold it, 'whoo.* He takes the picture.

BONNIE: *Mmm!*

CLYDE: *How about that?*

Quite suddenly, HAMER, whose simmering intensity we should be more sensitive to than the gang is, spits on BONNIE. BONNIE half-screams in disgust, but CLYDE is on top of HAMER in a flash, half-strangling on his own fury. He pulls HAMER off the fender by the handcuffs, spinning him around crazily like a lasso. HAMER is literally ricochetted off the car by the force, and, with CLYDE hanging on by the cuffs, plummets down the embankment to the edge of the water below. Both men wrestle back and forth. CLYDE gets on top of him. Meanwhile, BUCK has rushed down near the water, trying to stop CLYDE.

BUCK: *Hold up there . . . Wait, wait! I got the picture.*

BLANCHE off-screen: *Buck, stop it! Buck, stop it!*

CLYDE shoves HAMER forward and he starts to topple. He lands with a splash in the lake; CLYDE leaps on top of him.

BUCK frantic: *I got the picture!*

CLYDE pulls him by the handcuffs and tries to hurl him out further into the water. He hitches HAMER over a mouldy skiff, knocking aside the oars. BUCK, still intervening and shouting, is heaved into the water by CLYDE. CLYDE upends

HAMER into the skiff and kicks it spinning.

BONNIE shouting off-screen: *We're gonna put that picture . . . in every paper in the country!*

BUCK and CLYDE start pushing the boat through the water.

BLANCHE off-screen: *Buck! Stop it now! Please! Stop it!*

BUCK and CLYDE are chest-deep, breathing heavily.

CLYDE yelling to HAMER: *We got you, hear! We got you! We got you! Hey! We got you.*

HAMER battered and handcuffed, stares back from the lazily spinning skiff as it drifts into the distance.

CLYDE off-screen: *You just sit there for a while.*

BUCK drags CLYDE back up toward the bank.

BUCK: *I got the picture!*

HAMER, in the distance, stares with mindless malice at the hysterical specter of CLYDE screaming his madness across the water.

CLYDE still yelling off-screen: *We got you. We gonna use you, boy!*

BUCK off-screen: *Hey, come on.*

CLYDE yelling at the edge of the water: *We got you!*

INTERIOR BANK (DAY)

Inside a small town bank. In contrast to the previous inept bank robbery scene, this one goes admirably well, the gang performing slickly and without a hitch. As they enter, all dressed very smartly, CLYDE makes a general announcement to everyone.

CLYDE: *Ehh, good afternoon. This is the Barrow Gang.*

The people turn and freeze.

CLYDE: *Now if everybody will just take it easy, nobody will get hurt.*

CLYDE covers the door. BONNIE and BUCK go to the tellers' cages to get the money. BUCK takes a running jump, leaps up onto the top of the high desk grille, and over the other side to empty out the cash drawers.

Cut to BONNIE who motions to a woman to fill the sack.

Cut to CLYDE standing near the door, training his guns on the entire bank. A FARMER stands a few feet away, some bills clutched in his hand.

CLYDE: *Is that your money or the bank's?*

101

FARMER : *Mine.*
CLYDE : *All right, you keep it, then.*
    Across the floor, the BANK GUARD in the corner takes advantage of CLYDE's distraction to go for his gun. CLYDE spots it and fires a shot that just knocks the BANK GUARD's hat off without harming him.

EXTERIOR BANK
Cut to C.W. waiting outside the bank. He looks startled by the noise of the shot.
BLANCHE waits inside the car.

INTERIOR BANK
CLYDE to the GUARD, who has practically frozen in fear : *Next time I'll aim a little lower.*
    They finish robbing the bank. They start to exit. Near the door stands a guard with his hands raised. He wears sun glasses of the period with steel rims and round lenses. As they leave, BUCK snatches the sun glasses from the guard's head.

BUCK: *Take a good look, Pop. I'm Buck Barrow. We're the Barrow boys.*

An alarm bell starts to ring off-screen. BUCK, CLYDE and BONNIE back out the door.

EXTERIOR BANK

The gang runs wildly down the steps into the street where the car waits, motor running. As they leap into the car, BUCK throws the sun glasses into BLANCHE'S lap.

BUCK: *Happy birthday, hon'!*

They zoom off. Shots are heard. BONNIE, BUCK and CLYDE begin firing at the bank guards who are pursuing them. The guards fire back. BLANCHE is sitting in the back seat with her fingers stuck tightly in her ears, eyes shut, trying to overcome her panic. A funny image, but one that also awakens pity. The next sequence is carried out in cross-cutting. Flatt and Scruggs "Foggy Mountain Breakdown" on the soundtrack.

THE STREET IN FRONT OF THE BANK

A police car pulls up and the excited crowd gestures in the

direction of the departed gang.

VARIOUS VOICES : *Hurry . . . Hurry . . .*

BANK GUARD : *It was the Barrow gang, Charlie, I think they're headed for Oklahoma.*

INTERIOR GANG CAR (DAY)

The gang is exchanging gunshots with the police who are not far behind. CLYDE is at the wheel with BONNIE beside him. The others behind.

INTERIOR BANK

The gang has left a legacy of celebrity behind. We see the BANK GUARD whose hat was shot off being interviewed by a reporter. He is seated in a chair, his shirt open at the collar and a woman teller is fanning him.

BANK GUARD enjoying the limelight : *There I was, starin' square into the face of death!*

A photographer steps in. The BANK GUARD hurriedly buttons up his collar and smiles as the flashbulb goes off.

EXTERIOR GANG'S CAR

Still speeding along a country road. Followed by the police cars.

INTERIOR POLICE CAR

Two men in police uniforms following BONNIE and CLYDE. One of them fires a shot at the gang's car.

EXTERIOR GANG'S CAR

The chase continues. Shooting back and forth.

INTERIOR BANK

The FARMER is talking about BONNIE and CLYDE to the reporter. It is as though he'd just had contact with a portion of the true cross.

FARMER gravely : *And all's I can say is, they did right by me, and I'm bringin' me a mess o' flowers to their funeral.*

EXTERIOR GANG'S CAR
Camera follows the car as it drives past some notices:
"OKLAHOMA BORDER 2 MILES" and "3 MILES TO
JOE'S DINER—THE BEST FOOD IN TEXAS". The car
follows the sign for Oklahoma.

EXTERIOR POLICE CAR
A police car follows closely behind, it skids on the corner,
taking one of the notices with it.

INTERIOR BANK
The BANK PRESIDENT and the BANK GUARD are posing for
that classic picture where both stand flanking a bullet hole
in the wall and point proudly at it. The flashbulb goes off.

EXTERIOR GANG'S CAR
It speeds past a sign that says "YOU ARE ENTERING
OKLAHOMA".

INTERIOR GANG'S CAR

C.W.: *Slow down, we're in Oklahoma now.*

They all sigh with relief.

EXTERIOR POLICE CAR

It passes the same sign and starts to slow down.

INTERIOR POLICE CAR

FIRST POLICEMAN, a young eager beaver type: *Aw, come on, let's catch 'em anyway!*

SECOND POLICEMAN: *I ain't gonna risk my life in Oklahoma.*

They turn back.

EXTERIOR ROADSIDE BY CORNFIELD

They get out, taking the various bags of money with them, and dump the lot on the ground. There is not an impressive amount of money.

CLYDE disappointed: *Ain't much, is it?*

BUCK commiseratingly: *Well, times is hard.*

CLYDE: *Well, let's get down to it.*

He begins dealing and splitting the money out to each member of the gang, as they gather around. He hands one to BUCK, then to BONNIE, then puts one down for C.W., then one for himself.

CLYDE as he deals: *Mr. Buck Barrow . . . Bonnie . . . C. W. Moss, Clyde . . .* He goes back to the first again and lays out another round: *Buck . . . Bonnie . . .*

TWO SHOT BLANCHE AND BUCK

BLANCHE looks fretful. She nudges BUCK and whispers to him.

BLANCHE: *I want my share. If Bonnie gets a share, I want . . .*

BUCK whispers back to her.

BUCK: *Huh, what you talking about?*

Meanwhile, CLYDE's counting still goes on.

BLANCHE: *Tell Clyde I want my share.*

BUCK: *All right, all right . . .* Very ill at ease in this position he has been forced into: *Uh, Clyde?*

CLYDE: *What?*

BUCK is clearly embarrassed.

106

BUCK: *Uh, what about Blanche here?*

Everyone reacts with stunned amazement at BLANCHE'S nerve in wanting to get her cut.

BONNIE incredulous: *WHAT?*

BLANCHE: *Well, why not?*

BLANCHE sees she has to rise to her own defence, and she rises to the occasion with spirit and verve.

BLANCHE: *Well, why not? I earn my share same as everybody. Well I coulda got killed same as everybody, and I'm wanted by the law same as everybody. Well, besides I coulda got snake bit sleepin' in them woods every night!* . . . building it up . . . *I'm a nervous wreck and that's the truth . . . and I have to take sass from Miss Bonnie Parker all the time. I deserve mine!*

BUCK is looking at CLYDE, his face full of weak smiles and embarrassment at his wife.

CLYDE raises his hand: *Hold on, Blanche, . . . hold your horses, Blanche. You're gonna get your share.*

BONNIE is livid but says nothing. CLYDE, the leader has decided. C.W. looks indignant, like a hog who's just been given a bath. CLYDE gathers up the notes and begins counting all over again in near silence.

BUCK trying to make a joke of it: *I married the preacher's daughter and she thinks she's still takin' up a collection.*

Everyone now laughs, but BLANCHE. She looks triumphant. CLYDE continues counting.

CLYDE: *Mrs. Buck Barrow.*

BLANCHE: *Thank you.*

BUCK to BLANCHE: *Now honey, don't spend it all in one place.*

BONNIE turns and stalks away from the car. After a moment CLYDE stops counting and moves after her. He's prepared for a fight, stands behind BONNIE, trying to gauge the degree of her hostility.

CLYDE, a little defensive: *Listen, now, honey, I guess I have to keep saying this: Blanche is married to Buck, and Buck is* family.

He waits expectantly.

BONNIE looks plaintively to CLYDE.

BONNIE: *My family could use some of that money.*

CLYDE: *Now you know them laws, been hangin' round your mama's house till all hours. It's too risky to go up there now.*

107

BONNIE : *But, where* can *we go now we rob the damn banks, what else do we do?*

CLYDE finds it difficult to answer.

CLYDE : *Well, what d'you want to do?*

Suddenly C.W. starts yelling.

C.W. : *Clyde! Clyde! Clyde!*

C.W. comes bounding over.

C.W. : *Clyde, there's a hole in the pan. We're losing oil. We got to swipe another car if we want to get anywhere. C'mon, look.*

He drags them over, slides under the car and scoops up a gooey handful of slick black oil which he holds before their faces.

EXTERIOR SUBURBAN STREET

A residential neighborhood on a suburban street. A rather well-to-do neighborhood. The camera is up on a porch of a white frame house, looking toward the street. On the porch, sitting in the swing in the left foreground are a man, EUGENE, and a woman, VELMA. She is about twenty-nine, he is about thirty-six. He is sitting with his back to us, embracing the woman. They are spooning, making low loving murmurs.

VELMA : *Eugene, stop that now! C'mon stop that, Eugene.*

We see in the distance two cars parked in front of the house. His and hers. Suddenly we see another car drive up (BONNIE and CLYDE) and somebody gets out. Then the whole gang gets out, ditches the one car and gets in one of the parked cars. All the while the couple on the porch is busy spooning. The car begins to roll slowly into the street. The woman notices.

VELMA : *Say, isn't that your car, Eugene?*

He looks and leaps from the swing, shouting :

EUGENE : *That's my car! Hey!*

They run down the front steps and stare dumbfounded.

EUGENE : *Hey! That's my car! Hey! That's my car!*

They run toward the second car, jump in and take off, giving chase.

INTERIOR VELMA'S CAR

The woman is driving (it's her car). The man is furious. They

108

continue driving, furious, the man cursing and muttering. We see through their wind-shield the other car way in the distance.

INTERIOR BONNIE AND CLYDE'S CAR
CLYDE is driving, everybody is laughing and chattering.
C.W.: *Hey, get a look at his face.*
BUCK: *Hey, they're coming after us.*
BONNIE: *C'mon, kick it in the pants.*
BLANCHE: *Those people?*
C.W.: *Yeah.*

INTERIOR VELMA'S CAR
EUGENE clenching his fists: *I gonna tear 'em apart. Those punks! Stealing a man's car! Right! Wait'll I get my hands on those kids, Velma. I'm gonna tear them apart.*
VELMA: *What if they have guns, Eugene?*
EUGENE realizing the possibility, suddenly stops being mad and turns chicken: *Listen, we better get the police and let them handle this.*

VELMA relieved : *Right.*
EUGENE : *All right, all right, now, turn around. Turn around and let's go back to town. Then we'll go get the sheriff.*

They are by now on a narrow dirt road and VELMA has to execute a U-turn. It takes her about seven cuts to turn the car around in the narrow space. They start back to town.

INTERIOR BONNIE AND CLYDE'S CAR

BUCK looks out the rear window.
BUCK : *They stopped chasin' us. Hey, they're turning around there.*

CLOSE-UP CLYDE

He is grinning mischievously.
CLYDE : *Let's take 'em.*

BUCK and C.W. laugh appreciatively at the reversal. CLYDE turns the car around. He performs the U-turn in the same narrow space in one, swift, smooth, beautiful turn.

INTERIOR THE OTHER CAR

VELMA looks in the rear view mirror and sees that now she is being chased.
VELMA : *Oh, my Lord, they're comin' after us.*
EUGENE in a panic : *Step on it, Velma, step on it!*
VELMA gasping : *We ... I ...*
EUGENE : *Velma, step on it, Velma. Step on it, Velma.*
VELMA screeching : *I am!*

WINDSCREEN BONNIE AND CLYDE'S CAR

The gang, seen through the windscreen.
BLANCHE : *What'd'you want to do that for, Clyde?*
BUCK : *C'mon, c'mon!*
BONNIE : *C'mon!*

INTERIOR VELMA'S CAR

VELMA jams the accelerator down to the floor. Through the rear window the other car can be seen chasing them.
EUGENE trying to keep calm : *Step on it, Velma. Step on it, Velma.*

The Barrow Gang is gaining on them.
VELMA gasping : *Oh!*

INTERIOR BONNIE AND CLYDE'S CAR
BUCK urging CLYDE on : *C'mon, c'mon. C'mon Clyde, c'mon!*
BONNIE off-screen : *We're getting 'em. We're getting 'em.*

INTERIOR VELMA'S CAR
EUGENE : *Velma, step on it, Velma! . . . Velma!*

EXTERIOR ROAD THE CHASE
BONNIE and CLYDE's car gaining on them, gaining on them, gaining on them and finally overtaking them, coming up and ahead, forcing them to the side of the road.

EXTERIOR ROAD VELMA'S CAR
Terrified, VELMA and EUGENE roll up their windows, lock their doors and huddle together. The Barrow gang pile out of their car and walk over, having a merry time. They surround the car and press their faces against the window, flattening their features, making menacing gestures at the shaking pair inside. We see this from the point of view of the man and woman inside the car. CLYDE pulls out a gun, makes as if to shoot, but he is kidding. They all laugh uproariously, especially BUCK who is delighted with CLYDE's prank. All of this we see in pantomime from inside the trapped car.

BONNIE : *Ain't they cute?*
BUCK : *Howdy . . . Hey, hey, what're you doing in there?*
BONNIE : *Hey! Uh, may we—uh, ma'am?*
BUCK : *Uh, woo-whoo. Ho, you all!*
BONNIE : *Look what we got here.*
CLYDE : *C'mon, get out! Get out of there, I said.*
    They come out, hands raised high, shaking with fear. They have practically turned to jelly.
CLYDE ordering them into the other car : *You want to go for a little ride in our new car?*
BLANCHE : *Oh my, can we all sit in there?*
CLYDE laughing : *C'mon.*
C.W. laughing : *Hey! Hey, I get to ride up in front now.*
VARIOUS VOICES : *Hurry up now. C'mon, c'mon. C'mon . . . Finally!*
BLANCHE whining : *Oh! There's not room for me in there.*

111

BONNIE : *Ah!*
CLYDE : *C'mon, honey.*

INTERIOR OTHER CAR
They get in and the gang gets in. Seven people are now jammed inside. CLYDE drives, BONNIE next to him, C.W. next to her. In the back, BLANCHE, then EUGENE with VELMA (of necessity) sitting on his lap, and then BUCK. As will be seen, the reason the Barrows have kidnapped the couple is simply that they wanted company. Living as they do, seeing only each other day after day, they long for diversion and new faces. So the atmosphere in the car will shortly change to one of friendliness and jollity, and it will get progressively more so in the series of cuts which advance the time. As the car starts up at the beginning, however, the man and woman are terrified.

BUCK : *What are your names?*

EUGENE hesitantly : *I'm Eugene Griz—I'm Eugene Grizzard.*

VELMA : *And I'm Velma Davis.*

BUCK just as friendly as he can be : *Well, we're the Barrow gang and that there's Clyde drivin' and I'm Buck, that's my wife Blanche, Bonnie Parker, C.W.*

The man and woman almost faint from fear; clutch at each other. The gang all laugh at this. VELMA and EUGENE begin to realize that they are not going to get hurt and that the Barrows are friendly to them.

BONNIE : *Oh now listen, now don't be scared or anything like that. Now it ain't like you was the law or anything like that. I mean you're just folks like us. That's all.*

EUGENE agreeing over-enthusiastically : *Yeah, yeah, that's the truth.*

CLYDE : *I expect you've been readin' about us.*

The man and the woman answer simultaneously with what they think is the right thing to say under the circumstances.

EUGENE : *Yes.*

VELMA : *Oh no.*

They glare at each other.

EUGENE meaningfully : *Yes. We have too.*

BONNIE laughing at the contretemps : *Well now, you two must be in love, I bet, huh?*

EUGENE and VELMA blush, get shy for a second. BONNIE smiles.

112

BUCK gleefully thrusting a shot gun at EUGENE : *Now boy, when you gonna marry the girl?*
BLANCHE : *Buck!*
    He chuckles heartily.
    VELMA bursts into tears.

INTERIOR CAR (LATER)
We are still driving, same positions, but some time has elapsed. The atmosphere is now completely convivial and the captives are enjoying their new friends. As the scene starts, BUCK is finishing his joke.
BUCK : *So, he gave her the milk, and she drank a little bit of it. And the next day he gave her some more and she, she drank a little more until one week goes by, see. And he brings her the milk and she drinks down every, every drop of it. And, she looks at her son and she calls him over and she says, "Son, whatever you do, don't sell that cow." ... Don't sell the cow!*
EUGENE : *Oh boy!*
    The couple laugh with great amusement, but everyone else in the car doesn't laugh—this is the tenth time they've heard the joke.

INTERIOR OF CAR
It is getting on toward evening. All are thoroughly relaxed and chatting.
EUGENE : *I'm from Wisconsin originally.*
    BUCK, EUGENE, VELMA and BLANCHE are getting on famously.
EUGENE : *Where the cheese comes from!*
VELMA laughing : *Oh, oh, but he just loves Texas now.*
EUGENE : *Oh.*
VELMA : *Don't you Eugene?*
EUGENE laughing : *"Don't sell that cow."*
BONNIE to VELMA : *Uh, how old are you, honey?*
VELMA : *I'm thirty-three.*
    A sudden look of surprise registers on EUGENE's face.

INTERIOR OF CAR (NIGHT)
It is now night. Everyone inside the car is eating. Apparently they stopped somewhere along the way for food. In the

crowded interior, it is like a party—food is being passed back and forth, laughter and gaiety, increasing warmth between the couple and the Barrows. The car has become a little society on wheels, dashing through the black night down the highway. Inside there is a small world of happiness and fun. BUCK is unpacking the food and passing sandwiches and drinks around the car.

BUCK : *There they go.*

EUGENE : *Thanks Buck.*

VELMA : *Now uh, now didn't I order some French fries?*

BUCK passing her some : *Yeah, you did. Here you are. Here y'are. Everybody, you want . . . Hey, wait a min . . .*

CLYDE : *Now, take it easy on them French fries, Velma. Ain't that right, Eugene?*

EUGENE studying his hamburger : *This isn't mine. I ordered mine well done. Who's got the other hamburger?*

CLOSE-UP C.W.
He has already taken a bite of his hamburger.

C.W. : *Oh, is this supposed to be yours?*

He extends the bitten burger to EUGENE.

FULL SHOT
EUGENE : *S'okay, forget it.*

BUCK chewing : *Haw! I'm havin' a good time! Aren't you glad we picked you up? Huh?*

EUGENE : *You're a grand host, Buck.*

CLYDE laughing : *Maybe y'all ought to join up with us.*

That idea strikes everyone as being very amusing.

EUGENE laughing : *Oh, oh, ho, boy, they would sure be surprised to hear that back home.*

VELMA : *What would . . . What would Bill and Martha say if they heard that?*

She roars with laughter.

EUGENE roars with laughter : *Lordy, they would have a fit.*

BONNIE laughing : *Hey, what d'you do, anyhow?*

EUGENE as his laugh begins to fade : *I'm an undertaker.*

Suddenly everyone freezes. A shudder, as if the cold hand of death had suddenly touched the occupants of the car. The

114

atmosphere changes to cold, deadly, fearful silence in exactly one second. It is a premonition of death for the Barrows, and they react accordingly, BONNIE especially.

CLOSE-UP BONNIE
BONNIE tautly, in a flat voice : *Get them out of here.*

EXTERIOR ROAD
The car brakes to a sudden stop. The rear door is opened, VELMA and EUGENE are flung out into the darkness. The car drives off into the lonely night.

From this point on, the audience should realize that death is inevitable for the Barrow gang, that it follows them always, that it waits everywhere. It is no longer a question of whether death will come, but when it will.

EXTERIOR CORNFIELDS BONNIE (MORNING)
BONNIE is walking through a cornfield. She seems far away, stalking off, looking neither to right nor left, carrying a bundle of clothes in a brown paper sack. The voices of CLYDE and BLANCHE can be heard calling her on the soundtrack.

EXTERIOR CORNFIELDS CLYDE
Camera is moving with CLYDE as he tears his way through the brush, snagging his clothes, calling BONNIE's name. CLYDE's search is so desperate here that for a moment we might think he is fleeing from something rather than looking for something. In a moment he emerges onto the road. The car, with C.W. driving, and BUCK and BLANCHE beside him, is patrolling slowly up ahead of him.

BLANCHE : *I don't see her, Clyde.*

CLYDE spots the car and runs toward it. Hold at this angle until he catches up with it and runs along beside it.

MOVING SHOT CAR
CLYDE, now running along beside it, his head poked into the car, his face red and sweating.

CLYDE breathing heavily : *Where d'you think she could have gone, Buck?*

BUCK : *Boy, I dunno, I just dunno.*

115

CLYDE looks helplessly at his brother. He continues on foot, running along, scanning the fields—the car keeping up beside him as he runs, and we track before both car and CLYDE.

EXTERIOR CORNFIELDS
We see BONNIE walking through the maize fields She starts to run.

ANGLE THROUGH THE WINDSHIELD
CLYDE, has suddenly seen something. He begins gesticulating wildly.
CLYDE : *There! Bonnie! Bonnie! Bonnie!*
He starts running off into the cornfield.
As he does we see BONNIE, her yellow hair unmistakable even at this distance. She's far away in the cornfield. CLYDE screams, "BONNIE". She pays no attention.

ANGLE ON CORNFIELD
As CLYDE gets closer, BONNIE herself suddenly breaks into flight. There is a real chase where they each try to get the advantage. CLYDE is so exhausted from his run that he has real trouble cornering her as they maneuver up and down the rows of corn. Finally CLYDE catches up with her as she trips and falls.
CLYDE : *Bonnie!*
BONNIE : *Leave me alone!*
CLYDE holding her, kissing her frantically : *Where you going?*
BONNIE : *Get away!*
CLYDE : *Bonnie!*
BONNIE : *Go . . .*
CLYDE : *Honey!*
    CLYDE is on his knees beside her. He holds her tightly. They are both crying.
CLYDE : *Bonnie!*
BONNIE : *Oh.*
CLYDE : *Bonnie.*
BONNIE : *Oh, I want, I wanna see my mama. I wanna see my mama.*

CLYDE : *Please, honey, don't never leave me without saying nothing.*
BONNIE : *Clyde. But, no, but, Clyde, listen to me. Clyde, please. N-now listen . . . I mean it. I wanna—been thinking about my mama, and she, she—she's getting so old and I, I wanna see her. Please, Clyde. Please.*

CLYDE nods understandingly.
CLYDE : *You'll see her . . .* Enormously relieved, kissing her : *You'll see her.*

They remain clasped together.

EXTREME LONG SHOT THE CORNFIELD
The two of them holding one another far off in the distance. Dissolve to :

EXTERIOR SIDE OF A ROAD SAND TIP (DAY)
Very long shot of three or four cars parked on the side of a road in Texas. There are a lot of people gathered around, but the sound is an indistinct mixture of talk, laughter, etc. There

follows a quick montage of cuts which isolate specific moments in the family reunion, thereby implying the entire tone of the proceedings. The sense of family pervades. Everything seems slightly muffled, hazy, dream-like.

MONTAGE BONNIE'S MOTHER
Bonnie's Mother, an old woman.

MONTAGE BONNIE AND MOTHER
Her Mother grabs her and hugs her and cries.

MONTAGE C.W.
C.W. is standing guard on a sand-dune, with a shot gun.

MONTAGE BONNIE AND SISTER
Bonnie's Sister is standing behind a small boy. Bonnie kneels down beside him and holds the child's hand.
Bonnie : *Would you look at him. He just don't remember me. He'll get used to me, won't he?*

SISTER : *We been cuttin' and pastin' everything we could find about you in the papers.*

She shows them a scrapbook of clippings. CLYDE, BONNIE, BUCK and BLANCHE all look at the scrapbook. We see a page of it, showing a newspaper article with the photographs the gang took back at the motel.

BUCK : *Hey, hey, Clyde, there's the shot I took of you. Came out real fine, didn't it?*

MONTAGE BONNIE'S MOTHER
She stands alone. A frail old woman with her hands clasped against her skirt.

MONTAGE BONNIE AND SISTER
They are sitting on the running board of the car. BONNIE tidies her hair then turns to see her Sister's expression. They embrace.

MONTAGE BONNIE AND CLYDE AND MAN
BONNIE and CLYDE are posing for a comic snapshot. A silly looking male relative is posing, pointing a gun at them. They have their hands in the air and are grinning broadly. (The effect should be funny and simultaneously frightening.)

MONTAGE TWO SMALL BOYS
They are playing at the top of the sand-dune. One of them pretends to shoot the other, who falls and rolls down the dune. BONNIE is at the bottom of the dune. She helps him up and he runs away giggling.

MONTAGE BONNIE AND MOTHER
They are embracing.

MONTAGE BUCK AND SMALL BOY
BUCK is sitting with a little four-year-old on his knee bouncing him up and down and singing. Both are having a fine time.

BUCK : *"Horsey! get yer tail up, yer tail up, yer tail up. Horsey! get yer tail up. Why don't you make it rise?"*

119

MONTAGE THE FAMILY
They are gathered around a picnic spread. One of the men says grace.

FAMILY MEMBER: *Oh, Lord, we thank you for the safety of our loved ones. And the food we are about to receive. Amen.*

MONTAGE C.W.
C.W. standing guard. CLYDE brings him his lunch.

MONTAGE FAMILY PICNIC FAVORING CLYDE, MOTHER AND BONNIE
CLYDE, in his best theatrical manner has been playing host in the sand pile, perhaps using some sort of towel across the arm or around the middle. The party is beginning to break up now as used paper plates and crumpled napkins are blowing across the sand and the group is finishing up on Eskimo pie.

VARIOUS VOICES: *Bye, Clyde. Bye bye. You'll be careful. We're gonna miss you, now.*

BONNIE'S UNCLE rising: *Where y'all headed to from here, Clyde?*

CLYDE right back : *This point we ain't headin' to nowheres. We're just runnin' from.*

CLYDE laughs, in fine spirits.

REACTION BONNIE
She doesn't.

BONNIE'S SISTER off-screen : *Tom, Tom! We're goin' home. Little Tom? Mathew, fetch Little Tom.*

BONNIE coming over to her Mother : *Mama? . . . Why don't you stay a little while longer, huh? Okay?*

BONNIE takes off a chain with a pendant she is wearing round her neck.

BONNIE : *Listen, I want you to have this.*

BONNIE'S SISTER off-screen : *Come on, boys.*

BONNIE'S UNCLE off-screen : *Come on, you little rollers, we gotta go home.*

BONNIE puts the chain over her Mother's head and arranges it around her neck.

BONNIE to CLYDE : *Clyde, sugar . . . Listen, make mama stay a while yet.*

BONNIE turns with increased urgency to her Mother who has turned to CLYDE. He gives her a big, boyish hug.

MOTHER : *You know, Clyde, I read about y'all in the papers and I jes' get scared.*

CLYDE ignoring BONNIE, as does Mother, ebulliently, even joshing : *Now, Mrs. Parker, don't you believe what you read in all them newspapers! That's the laws talking there. They want us to look big so they gonna look big when they catch us.*

He knows he's stumbled onto the wrong thing, but he bounces right along — it's his style.

CLYDE : *And they ain't goin' catch us. 'Cause I'm even better at runnin' than I am at robbin' banks. Shoot, if we done half that stuff they say we done in them papers, we'd be millionaires by now, wouldn't we?* He turns to BONNIE who continues to stare at her Mother : *Look I ain't gonna risk my little girl here, just to make money, uncertain as times are. Why I knowed of a job . . . To*

BONNIE : *You remember, remember the time? . . . Why, I could have, we could have done $2,000 just as easy as pie. And I, I pulled up outside there and I saw them laws . . . and I said to myself,*

121

I said, "Bonnie could get hurt here." So we just drove right on and I let that money lay.

He waits for a response, as does BONNIE. BONNIE's Mother smiles, a little abstractedly.

MOTHER : *Maybe you know the way with her then. I'm just an old woman and I don't know nothin' . . .*

She trails off, looking nowhere in particular. CLYDE takes her reaction to mean that he's overwhelming her with his confidence, and continues to pour it on.

CLYDE : *Mrs. Parker. But Mrs. Parker, this here is the way we know best how to make money. But we going to be quittin' all this as soon as hard times is over, I can tell you that. Why, just the other night, me and Bonnie were talking, and uh, we were talking about the time we were going to settle down . . . and get us a home. And, uh, uh, she says to me . . . She says, "You know, I couldn't bear to live more'n' three miles from my precious mother." Now, how do you like that, Mother Parker?*

BONNIE's Mother has undergone a funny sort of transformation during CLYDE's speech — as if something had suddenly come into focus before the old woman's eyes.

MOTHER : *I don't believe I would. I surely don't . . . To BONNIE : You try to live three miles from me and you won't live long, honey . . . To CLYDE . . . You'd best keep runnin' Clyde Barrow, and you know it . . . Bye, baby.*

She hugs BONNIE who can barely respond. We move in for a close-up of BONNIE as her various relatives, young and old, move toward the cars, waving and shouting cheery goodbyes. As the cars leave, they wave to the gang who are standing motionless on the sand.

FAMILY MAN : *Bye, you all.*

They all wave goodbye.

INTERIOR PLATTE CITY MOTEL BEDROOM
PLATTE CITY, IOWA C.W. — BUCK — BLANCHE —
CLYDE
A naked lightbulb (the lampshade has been removed) glares down on C.W.'s chest—where a pair of blue-birds have been tattooed with a rococo flourish. BUCK is vastly amused. He examines it closely. C.W., who is wearing a gas mask, sits

back like some docile animal, submitting to inspection.

BUCK: *Look, who is this here, is this your girlfriend?* C.W. shakes his head. BUCK spells out the word: *"L-O-V-E."*

BONNIE tries, against heavy odds, to file and trim her nails in a corner of the room. The odds are CLYDE on a yuke, BUCK and BLANCHE gathered around C.W. who sits in the only stuffed chair in the room. Their raucousness is clearly shattering to BONNIE who, at a key moment in the scene, ends up spearing her cuticle with a file, spurting a little blood and a lot of temper.

BUCK: *Well, whose idea was it to get bluebirds?*

C.W. pointing to BONNIE: *Bonnie picked it out.*

BUCK: *Bonnie, uh?*

C.W.: *Day after we robbed the armory.*

BUCK calling BLANCHE over: *Come over here. I want you to touch something here.*

BLANCHE: *Oh, no, Daddy.*

BUCK: *Now, I want you to just touch it right, right there.* BLANCHE stares fascinated as one of C.W.'s pectoral muscles contracts and the wings flutter : *Come on. There. You see.*

BLANCHE squeals with amusement. BUCK takes BLANCHE's hand and places it on the bluebirds. BLANCHE, titillated, squeals with delight.

REACTION BONNIE

Startled by BLANCHE's squeal, she digs the file into her cuticle. She winces in pain.

BONNIE with barely controlled rage : *What are you all doin'?*

INTERIOR MOTEL BEDROOM GROUP SHOT FAVORING BONNIE

BUCK laughing : *Sweet and sour!*

BONNIE with phoney patience : *Why — why don't you all go into your own cabin if you want to play with C.W.? Huh?*

NEW ANGLE MOTEL BEDROOM

BLANCHE : *What's the matter with you now, besides your nasty disposition?*

CLYDE sees something coming : *Now wait a minute, Blanche. Wait a minute now.*

BUCK who doesn't want to be victimized by BONNIE's temperament: *Why should she wait?*

CLYDE : *N-now listen to me.*

BUCK : *No!*

BLANCHE : *She just never fails to . . . share with us.*

BUCK : *I mean, why should she have to wait?*

CLYDE angrily : *Hold on, now.*

BONNIE sits impassively, filing her nails.

CLYDE peacemaking : *Look, I saw a chicken place a few miles back. Who wants to get some food?*

BLANCHE : *I certainly do. I'm sick to death of sittin' around here.*

BUCK : *Why you can't even drive the car, honey.*

C.W. reluctantly : *Well, I'll go.*

C.W. makes as if to move out with BLANCHE. BUCK rises to go next door.

C.W. : *What do you all want?*

CLYDE : *Just get us five chicken dinners.*

BUCK : *Hey, get some dessert there too, some peach ice cream, or*

124

somethin', will you?

He grins and pats his stomach. All finally exit, leaving BONNIE and CLYDE alone.

EXTERIOR CAR AND STREET (DUSK)
C.W. and BLANCHE go out. We go with them. They get in the car and drive off. BUCK enters his cabin.

INTERIOR MOTEL BEDROOM BONNIE AND CLYDE
Everyone has left, they are alone. There is a beat of silence. BONNIE turns away from CLYDE and collapses on the bed.
BONNIE eyes brimming: *Oh, baby, I got the blues so bad . . .*
CLYDE moves behind her, begins to rub her thighs. There is something very delicate about the way he touches her; it suggests CLYDE's sensitivity to her mood rather than any degree of physical intimacy.
CLYDE: *Well, is it what your mama said?*
BONNIE: *What mama? She's, she's just an old woman now . . . I don't have no mama . . . No family either.*
BONNIE rolls over, on her back. She stares up at CLYDE, tears running down her cheeks.
CLYDE: *Hey, I'm your family.*
She raises her head, frowning. He smiles and nods. Her eyes brimming with tears, she starts to sit up. She wraps her arms around CLYDE's middle, and snuggles into him, like a child. He holds her tightly. Neither we nor CLYDE can see BONNIE's face now, and her voice is muffled by his chest.
BONNIE sobbing quietly: *You know, when we started out, I thought we was really goin' somewhere. But this is it. We're just goin', huh?*
She has addressed this last question directly to CLYDE, but there is nothing rhetorical about it — it is a real question. CLYDE doesn't answer for a moment. Then:
CLYDE quite simply: *I-I love you.*
It's the first time he's said it to her, and BONNIE is overwhelmed. She smiles and draws his hand toward her face . . .

INTERIOR CAR BLANCHE AND C.W.
BLANCHE, her tense and agitated self growing increasingly

more so lately, lights a fresh cigarette off the butt of the one she has been smoking.

C.W. conversationally : *You sure are smokin' a lot lately.*

BLANCHE quick to take offense, snaps : *So what?*

C.W. : *Nothin'.*

BLANCHE, sick of it all, drops her head in her hand with a sigh.

BLANCHE : *Oh, Lord . . .*

C.W. looks at her, finally decides to say something that occurs to him.

C.W. : *Whyn't you go back to your pa's house?*

BLANCHE, it's been her dream : *Oh, if only I could! If I could only do that one thing! Oh, there's no tellin' how all this happened. I was a preacher's daughter.*

C.W. : *What church was your pa affiliated with?*

BLANCHE much more interested in talking about herself : *Baptist . . . He thought the world of Buck, my daddy did. Even though Buck was serving time in jail. He forgave him 'cause he paid his debt to society.*

C.W. : *We were Disciples of Christ.*

INTERIOR FRIED CHICKEN CAFE

A lunch counter sweeps down the center of the screen. We are at one end of the counter. In the foreground, a Deputy sits drinking coffee, absorbed in his cup. In the background, at the other end of the counter, by the exit door, BLANCHE and C.W. are being handed their order by the counterman.

BLANCHE : *Hey, I ain't got no money. Gimme some, will you?*

The Deputy turns his head and looks over there. C.W. opens his jacket to reach in his pocket for some money. As he opens his coat, his gun is clearly seen tucked in his pants. Camera zooms in to tight close-up of the gun.

CLOSE SHOT DEPUTY

His face is tense. Sound of door closing shut, as C.W. and BLANCHE leave.

DEPUTY into the café pay telephone : *Get me Sheriff Smoot on the phone. Yeah.*

126

EXTERIOR PLATTE CITY MOTEL (NIGHT)

A dim light is coming from two of the cabin windows. The beginning of an Eddie Cantor song is heard on the sound-track and continues through the following scene.

INTERIOR BUCK'S CABIN

BUCK and BLANCHE are sleeping peacefully in their cabin.

INTERIOR THE OTHER CABIN

C.W. sleeps in the leather easy chair while BONNIE is trying on a new outfit, showing it off to CLYDE.

BONNIE quietly: *That's more like it. Look how much better it fits since I took it up.*

EXTERIOR PLATTE CITY MOTEL

Outside, everything seems very dark and very quiet. Ranged across the lawn are six police cars; loaded with peace officers. A man comes out and, gun drawn, walks cautiously over to the room on the right — BUCK and BLANCHE's. He knocks loudly on the door.

INTERIOR BUCK'S CABIN

There is a knock on the door. They sit bolt upright in bed. Before BUCK can say anything, BLANCHE puts her hand over his mouth to shut him up.

BLANCHE calling out: *The men are on the other side.*

EXTERIOR PLATTE CITY MOTEL

The lawman moves on to the next cabin where there is a light shining.

The lawmen, among them the Deputy from the café, edge their way across the lawn, past the first garage, past the second. Before they reach the door of BONNIE and CLYDE's cabin a shot rings out.

INTERIOR MOTEL

BONNIE and CLYDE duck down as the bullet hits the mirror, shattering it. C.W. wakes up and grabs a sub-machine gun. They are all bent low as the firing begins.

EXTERIOR MOTEL
We see a blinding light rolling up in a space between six cars. It is an armored truck, with mounted guns and spotlight, advancing toward the cabin. The firing continues.

INTERIOR MOTEL
CLYDE breaks a lightbulb, plunging everything into darkness. C.W. is firing through the window. CLYDE is firing a Browning Automatic.

EXTERIOR MOTEL
The lawmen blast their shotguns. Bursts of sub-machine gun fire from the cabin windows. Two of the lawmen fall to the ground, as others run back for cover.

INTERIOR MOTEL
BONNIE comes running up, screaming:
BONNIE: *C.W.! C.W.! Grenades!*

EXTERIOR MOTEL

Sound of gunshots coming from everywhere, piercing light. Bursts of fire come from the armored truck.
A lawman falls to the ground, shot from bullets fired by Bonnie and Clyde.
Quick shots of C.W., Clyde, Bonnie and the Sheriff all firing.

INSIDE THE GARAGE

Clyde must get into the garage to get to the car. They must escape. All they can do is escape, and all they have is that one car in the closed garage. His gun already firing (automatic clip) before he gets there, Clyde in a crouch runs to the garage door, flings it open and runs to the car. He is standing by the car firing the Browning Automatic. Continuous firing still comes from the law. The garage door is shaking from the impact of the bullets, shattering it. Clyde begins to get the car out: one hand on the wheel, one hand shooting, he rolls the car out of the garage. The battle rages on all sides.

EXTERIOR BUCK'S CABIN

BUCK and BLANCHE have come out, holding a double bed mattress in front of them for protection. This makes their running awkward — the mattress is heavy and BUCK is firing with the other hand.

EXTERIOR MOTEL

BONNIE and C.W. come charging out of their cabin, guns blazing away. C.W. fires the Thompson sub-machine gun, BONNIE fires two pistols with automatic clips. BONNIE makes for the car while C.W. lobs a grenade at the armored truck. It explodes. Lawmen duck to avoid the blast.

CLYDE hustles BONNIE inside the car. One cop is hit and he falls. C.W. continues firing his machine gun. Voices are heard shouting.

MAN : *Bring the car around there . . . the little guy.*

They all seem to be firing at C.W.

BLANCHE carries the front end of the mattress, BUCK the back with one hand, the other firing his gun. They get halfway to the car and BUCK is hit, shot in the head. He falls to the ground; BLANCHE and the mattress fall too, since she has lost balance. Both are under the mattress.

BLANCHE screaming : *No! Buck!*

At this moment, the gang's car bursts out of the garage. CLYDE dashes out of the car and drags BUCK into the back seat. BLANCHE follows, hysterical. BONNIE covers them. All guns on all sides are still firing. They fling themselves into the car and from a standing start, the car starts out at 60 mph down the driveway. One of the lawmen stands blocking the way with a double-barreled rifle, but the car keeps coming, about to run him down. He jumps out of the way and fires at the side. The glass cracks and we see BLANCHE fling a hand to her face, which is bloody. A piece of glass has lodged in her eye. We hear her scream. The horn is blasting. C.W., who has been covering them, jumps onto the running board as the car drives away into the night.

INTERIOR THE CAR

Swerving madly. CLYDE manages to keep it on the road. They

drive away.

EXTERIOR STREET
The police run back to their cars to give chase, calling out to each other, unable to believe that the gang could possibly have got away.

INTERIOR CAR
It is speeding down the highway. Packed inside this car right now is more sheer human misery and horror than could be believed. It is hell in there, hell and suffering and pain. The car is a complete mess. C.W. is sobbing. Everyone is hysterical. BLANCHE is shrieking with pain and concern for BUCK. BUCK is alternating between groaning and passing out completely. BONNIE is yelling at everybody to shut up. Only CLYDE, driving with both hands clenched on the wheel, is silent. The car is doing 90.

BLANCHE : *He's dyin'! He's dyin'!*
C.W. : *Gimme a gun, please! Somebody, gimme a gun. I don't*

have a gun! Listen!

BONNIE : *Now stop that! You gone crazy? What're you doin'?*

CLYDE's face is bathed in sweat as he concentrates on the driving.

CLYDE hopelessly : *Oh no!*

BONNIE : *You guys be quiet! Please be quiet! We're trying to get out.*

EXTERIOR SUBURBAN STREET (NIGHT)

The car from the outside, a half-hour later. They have eluded the police. They are barreling down the road at top speed on a nice suburban street with proper homes. It is the middle of the night, utter silence. CLYDE stops the car, points to a car in a driveway — is is a beautiful, shiny new and expensive automobile. C.W. runs out, runs up the driveway, peers inside, gets in, quietly backs it down the driveway and pulls behind the gang's bullet-riddled getaway car. Suddenly they both zoom off down the road together.

INTERIOR THE NEW CAR

C.W. driving alone. He is crying, mumbling, wiping his eyes and nose with one hand while he controls the wheel with the other.

INTERIOR GANG CAR

BLANCHE is cradling BUCK's head in her arms, weeping.

BLANCHE : *It didn't happen, Daddy, it didn't happen. I know it didn't happen.*

BONNIE : *Blanche, stop that!*

EXTERIOR RING OF FIRE (NIGHT)

A wide field in the country. This is Dexter, Iowa. It's quiet. We see, in a long shot that takes in everything, that this is a meadow surrounded by a ring of trees, a dense forest that circles them. The meadow, however, is large.

The two cars drive into the middle of the field, headlights on. They stop and the Barrow gang get out. They are in horrible shape — we can finally have a look at them. Half-dressed in their pajamas, bloody, dirty, in tatters. Those that can stagger

132

out do so, others are carried. A far shot of all this.

CLOSER SHOT

Moving closer to them, we see CLYDE and C.W. lay BUCK
down on the ground. CLYDE begins to administer to his wounds
as best he can, mostly just wiping him off. BUCK is semi-
conscious. All are in a semi-daze. BLANCHE falls to her knees,
still clutching her eyes. She is totally hysterical.

BLANCHE : *I'd rather go to jail than go on like this.*
She continues moaning, praying and sobbing.

TWO SHOT BONNIE and C.W.

BONNIE walks over to the group, looking at BUCK. C.W. goes
over to her.

C.W. : *He ain't got a chance. Half his head's blown off.*
Camera pulls back to take in BLANCHE.

BLANCHE : *Oh God! Oh God! It . . . Dear Lord! It's happened.
Please help us!*

BUCK groaning : *Blanche! Blanche!*

BLANCHE : *And Buck'll never do anything wrong again in his life.*
Screaming : *My eyes! I think I'm blind! My eyes, the light hurts
so bad . . . the light hurts so bad.*

BONNIE walks over to the car and comes back with the sunglasses BUCK had given BLANCHE.

CLYDE has knelt down to the side of BUCK, taking BUCK's hand
and with his other hand has begun smoothing BUCK's hair
back, away from the wound.

BUCK groaning : *Clyde . . . gimme a . . . Clyde, Clyde . . .*

Moving BLANCHE out of the glare of the headlights BONNIE
helps her put the glasses on. BONNIE now has an arm around
BLANCHE, and BLANCHE shivers into her gracefully. BONNIE
is a little repelled by BLANCHE, but comforts her out of genuine
feeling for her.

BONNIE : *Here, hon', here. Here.*

BLANCHE clinging : *Tell Clyde to get him to a doctor, Bonnie.
We're dyin'.*

BONNIE looks silently up to CLYDE. CLYDE is looking dumbly
down at his mangled brother.

BONNIE gently, knowing CLYDE will not, cannot answer BLANCHE :

133

Buck can't be moved, now, hon'.

BLANCHE's answer to this is hysterical sobbing, burying herself into BONNIE, mumbling half-coherent, muffled prayers between the sobs.

WITH BUCK AND CLYDE
BUCK struggles to sit up.
BUCK screaming : *Clyde! ... Clyde! ... Clyde! ...*
CLYDE : *Right here, boy.*
BUCK : *I believe I lost my shoes . . . Clyde. I think the dog got 'em . . .*

He lapses into unconsciousness again. CLYDE has begun to cry a little. He continues to smoothe back BUCK's hair with ritualistic regularity.

WIDE ANGLE
Camera pulls away, way back to the wide shot of the entire field, showing the group in the center of the darkness, lit by the headlights.
Match dissolve into early dawn, camera still on the wide shot. The field is lighter, though the trees still loom blackly around it. The two cars, one almost a shattered wreck, the other bright and shiny and new, are parked in the center. The sky is light, but the trees cast a dark shadow on the field. The gang is just sitting around. BLANCHE weeping next to BUCK, C.W. sitting on the running board of the car, staring. BONNIE standing and smoking. CLYDE still with BUCK.
All is quiet.

EXTERIOR WOODS (DAWN)
From the edge of the woods, a man in a white shirt emerges from behind a tree. The camera swings abruptly to get him. He calls out to the gang.
MAN : *Surrender!*
It is a total surprise. BONNIE, CLYDE, and C.W. get up and rush over to where BUCK is lying :
CLYDE : *Buck! The car! C'mon.*
MAN : *Surrender!*
The man lingers there for a moment — he looks strange,

white, luminous, like an apparition — and then he vanishes
into the woods. Silence, long enough to make you think it was
perhaps an illusion.

Without a word, all of the gang including the half-dead BUCK
(who is carried by CLYDE, C.W. and BONNIE) scramble for the
nearest car.

BONNIE : *Buck, keep low.*

They run throughout this battle, crouched, like animals —
their only thought, to get away, to escape. To fight it out
would be ludicrous.

From the moment the Barrows start in motion, there is shooting from the edge of the woods. We see them scrambling
toward the car, in an extreme long shot, surrounded by a
ring of smoke. There is a volley of gunfire — a noise so large
as to be almost an impossible sound — coming from the woods,
all around, everywhere. A ring of little white puffs of smoke
emerge from the woods; from every tree a puff of smoke. The
camera pans in a circle. Behind every tree is a man with a
gun. There are at least 150 people out there — peace officers,

135

farmers with hunting rifles, kids with squirrel guns, everyone who wanted to come along and catch BONNIE and CLYDE. Their number is so large because this time they want no possibility of the gang making what seemed to them super-natural escapes.

From this point on, the sound of the guns is unnaturally muffled on the sound track. We hardly hear them at all . . . it is like a dream.

INTERIOR OF THE CAR
All of them inside. CLYDE is at the wheel.

EXTERIOR CAR
Medium long shot of the car moving. We see the car looking for an avenue of escape. It veers toward a tree, a man steps out from behind the tree and fires, the car jerks and veers toward another tree, again a man steps out and fires and so on. The car performs its eccentric dance. The film should have the feeling of slow motion, as the car swerves and loops along the edge of the woods. Not once do any of the Barrows fire back. Another man steps out and aims.

INTERIOR CAR CLOSE-UP CLYDE AT THE WHEEL
CLYDE is shot in the arm. He grabs his arm in pain and loses control of the wheel.

EXTERIOR CAR
The car is out of control. It smashes into a tree stump.

INTERIOR CAR
From inside the smashed car, we peer out the window across the field and see the other car. The thought strikes the audience at the same time it strikes the gang — they must get to that car.

EXTERIOR CAR
They all get out.
BUCK off-screen : *I'll go get the car! . . . I'll get the car.*
CLYDE : *Buck!*

136

POSSE MEMBER enticingly off-screen : *Hey, Buck, this way!*
     BUCK sways about. A single shot hits him and sends him
     crashing to the ground. C.W. is trying to lead the way.
C.W. : *C'mon on through here!*
     BONNIE helps CLYDE away while he looks back toward
     BLANCHE kneeling over BUCK.
CLYDE overlapping : *Buck!*
POSSE off-screen : *They're headin' for the other car! Shoot it!*
POSSE off-screen : *Knock the hell out've it!*
     Medium shot of the second car sitting in the field, shining in
     the sun. The lawmen also realize what must be done — cut
     off this escape. Though BONNIE, CLYDE and C.W. are heading
     toward it, they suddenly train all their fire on the car rather
     than the gang.
     The car fills the frame of the screen. Bullets begin to hit it. It
     starts to quiver under the impact. For the next minute, we see
     the car die in front of our eyes. We see the beautiful machine
     fall to pieces — windows smash, tires are torn apart, body
     riddled. The death of the car is as painful to watch as the
     willful death of a human being. The execution is paced
     deliberately to show the ritualistic tempo of the destruction.

EXTERIOR WOODS
     The camera pulls back, way back and slightly above every-
     thing to reveal the entire field. On the left of the screen,
     BONNIE, CLYDE and C.W. are scrambling toward the edge of
     the woods. In the center BUCK and BLANCHE have taken cover
     behind a fallen log. In the foreground, police begin to emerge
     from the woods.
VOICE off-screen : *Hold your fire!*
     The camera moves in with them toward BUCK. BLANCHE is
     crying.
BLANCHE : *Daddy, don't die. Daddy don't die!*
     A shot rings out. BLANCHE goes beserk. Two men grab her
     and hold her as she writhes and cries. She is still wearing the
     sunglasses.
MAN : *I said hold your fire.*
     BLANCHE, struggling, screams as the men try to pull her away
     from BUCK.

BLANCHE : *Get away. Get away and leave him alone. He's dying.
Can't you see he's dying. Let me go! Daddy. You'll kill him. He's
dying. God, can't you see him dying. He's dead. Daddy. Daddy,
don't die, Daddy. Don't die. Oh, Daddy.*

BUCK, half-dead, is making a last feeble effort. He collapses on
the ground and dies. The posse gradually moves in and
surrounds them.

EXTERIOR WOODS AND STREAM BONNIE, CLYDE
AND C.W.
They have reached the edge of the woods. Camera tracks with
them as they run. From all around come the sounds of the
posse. The three get in through the pines and come finally to a
deep stream. They jump in and start across, running
awkwardly in chest-deep water. They are half-way across
when a policeman appears behind them, shooting.

CLOSE-UP BONNIE
She is struggling through the water. A bullet hits her in the

shoulder. We must see this bullet clearly, we must see it go in her flesh so that we can feel it.

Tight close-up of BONNIE's face as she screams. It is the first time she has been hurt, and the scream is pure animal pain.

EXTERIOR STREAM AND CORNFIELD

C.W. spins and shoots the policeman, who falls dead. CLYDE drags BONNIE out of the water and into a cornfield growing on the opposite bank, C.W. helping. He half-carries, half-runs with her into the cornfield, as it gets deeper and thicker. The three of them rest for a second.

CLYDE is working on pure adrenalin now. Leaving BONNIE and C.W. in the corn, he struggles to his feet.

EXTERIOR LONG SHOT FARMHOUSE AND CAR

In the distance, a farmhouse with a car parked in the driveway; it seems an interminable distance away. CLYDE runs toward it, stumbling and wounded, running through the corn until he is out of it and onto grass. After a few moments he disappears.

CLOSE-UP C.W. AND BONNIE
Obviously some time later. They both lie prostrate in the field waiting.

C.W. : *Maybe . . .*

BONNIE : *Shhh!*

They wait for another long moment, picking up only the tiniest sounds.

FARMHOUSE AND CAR
CLYDE is seen with the hood of the car open.

BONNIE AND C.W.
We hear the sound of an approaching car. Reaching the cornfield, CLYDE drives the car right through the corn, finally coming to a stop a few feet in front of C.W. and the semi-conscious BONNIE. CLYDE, bleeding from his shoulder quite heavily, and C.W. carry BONNIE into the back seat. CLYDE gets in beside BONNIE and C.W. drives off.

INTERIOR CAR SOME TIME LATER (NIGHT)
They have got away, but are still escaping. C.W. is driving. He is bare-chested. BONNIE and CLYDE, are both in the back seat, unconscious, covered with blood.

Dissolve to :

EXTERIOR ROAD WITH CAMPSITE (DAWN)
C.W. is driving down the road, hell for leather. He is nearing a campsite, where there are about six Oakie cars and pick-up trucks all loaded down, with a number of poor families seated around a campfire cooking. C.W. jams on the brakes. He gets out looking totally exhausted.

REACTION SHOT THE FACES OF THE OAKIES
They are looking at this sudden presence in their midst.

BACK TO C.W.
C.W. about to drop : *Can y'all spare us some drinkin' water?*

FULL SHOT EXTERIOR CAMPSITE

One MAN, the leader of the group, dips a cup of water and hands it to him.

MAN: *Who are you, boy?*

C.W.: *Name is Moss.*

C.W. gulps it down. He takes the rest over to the car where we see that BONNIE is unconscious, and CLYDE semi-conscious. C.W. holds the cup to BONNIE's lips. The Oakies begin to circle the car, peering into it suspiciously. Suddenly a MAN starts and his eyes open wide.

MAN in really hushed and reverent tones: *That's Clyde Barrow and Bonnie Parker.*

He stands there struck dumb, staring. Those of the others who have heard him begin to come over. Without a word they move quietly to the car and stare in.

LITTLE GIRL: *What happened to them?*

MAN: *Shhh. Hush.*

LITTLE GIRL: *They faintin'?*

MAN : *Sure 'nough.*

INTERIOR CAR
CLYDE is semi-conscious in the back seat. He looks up through half-closed eyes. BONNIE is still unconscious beside him.

EXTERIOR CAR
We see a woman pour a bowl of soup at the campfire and bring it to C.W. He accepts it. Children peer through the back window. C.W. finishes his cup of soup. He hands it and the cup of water back to the woman in the crowd.
Quietly, moving together, the Oakies step back. C.W. walks to the driver's seat, gets in and shuts the door. He starts up the car.
The people push a bit closer for a last look. CLYDE, unable to do more, nods his head in a barely perceptible gesture by way of saying "thank you" to the people.
GIRL : *Is that really Bonnie Parker?*
BOY : *Yeah.*

EXTERIOR MALCOLM MOSS' FARM (MIDDLE OF THE NIGHT)
The car pulls up outside the slightly ramshackled farm of C.W.'s father, in Arcadia, Louisiana. It sits, for a moment, in the dark. Then C.W. honks the horn. A few seconds pass, and the porch light comes on. MALCOLM MOSS comes out in his pajamas and peers into the darkness. He is a fat man with gray hair.
C.W. off-screen : *Daddy! Daddy!*
MALCOLM : *Who's there?*
C.W. : *C.W.*
MALCOLM : *Huh?*
C.W. : *Clarence.*
MALCOLM : *CLARENCE!*
C.W. : *Yeah!*
He runs down the steps, down the path to his son. They greet each other, hugging for a second, looking each other over.
MALCOLM : *Oh, it's good to see you, boy! Oh boy, it's good to see you!*

142

C.W. : *Come on Daddy.*

He holds C.W. at arm's length to study him, and suddenly he scowls at something he sees by the light of the porch.

MALCOLM suspiciously : *What's that on your chest, there?*

C.W. realizing what he means : *Tattoo Daddy. Come on.*

Puzzled, MALCOLM follows. He goes to the car and looks inside for a moment. He walks back to C.W.

C.W. : *You gotta help 'em.*

INTERIOR CAR

BONNIE is pale, unconscious, her face and neck covered with blood; CLYDE beside her, his shoulder red with blood.

EXTERIOR C.W. AND MALCOLM MOSS

MALCOLM looks horrified.

C.W. : *Help me get 'em in.*

MALCOLM : *What happened to them? Are you in trouble, son?*

C.W. : *Clyde Barrow and Bonnie Parker. Come on. Help me get 'em in.*

They go to the car and drag the unconscious BONNIE out and begin carrying her up to the house.

MALCOLM : *How come you mark yourself all up with that tattoo? What the hell made you do a damn fool thing like that? You hear me?*

They reach the house.

C.W. : *Just open the door, Dad.*

INTERIOR SHERIFF'S OFFICE IN DEXTER (DAY)

The SHERIFF and his DEPUTY are sitting at a table playing dominoes. HAMER has just arrived in the office and stands over them. He is dressed in his Ranger outfit and hat, and again he has that quality of sinister frenzy beneath his calm manner. His attitude towards these lawmen is sheer condescension, friendly only out of convention, really superior and contemptuous of lesser workers in his field. HAMER throws a pad down onto the dominoes game, messing it up.

They look up from their game. The SHERIFF picks up the pad, looking at it. It is one of the photographs of HAMER with

Bonnie and Clyde.

Hamer off-screen: *I come here to question Blanche Barrow.*

Deputy: *So you're the . . .* mispronouncing his name . . . *Frank Hammer.*

Hamer: Ham*er. I figger to have my picture took with them two just one more time . . .*

CLOSE SHOT NEWSPAPER

We see a newspaper story about Clyde. It reads: "WHERE IS HE? NO TRACE SINCE CLYDE FLED DYING BROTHER. Since his miraculous escape from law enforcement officers, Clyde Barrow has seemingly melted into thin air. Authorities are continuing the widespread search and are hopeful of uncovering new clues in the near future."

C.W.'s voice off-screen: *It says here Clyde fled his dying brother.*

Clyde's voice off-screen: *Where?*

Clyde's hand tears the newspaper, and we move to C.W.'s startled face.

EXTERIOR FRONT PORCH OF MOSS FARM (DAY)

They are on the porch. Clyde is standing over C.W., his arm in a sling.

Clyde: *What do they mean? Fled? How could I leave my brother to die when he was already dead when I left him? Fled!*

Bonnie and Malcolm are also on the porch. Bonnie's arm is in a sling. By this point in the film, Bonnie wears no make-up. Her face is thinner, more ascetic — both she and Clyde have been refined down to the pure essence of themselves, and it is reflected in the way they look. It is evident by Clyde's heavy indignation and Bonnie's attentiveness that both are well on the way to recovery.

Clyde continues: *Newspapers! While we're all lyin' around here, near dead, they has us holdin' up the Grand Prairie National Bank! Guess they hung that one on us just for luck. I tell you somethin'. As soon's we get well, we're gonna hold up that bank! We gonna take it!*

He breaks into a wicked grin, but then reels, catching himself on the porch railing. He's obviously dizzy from exertion and

144

anger. BONNIE starts — then sees CLYDE is in control — but she makes him sit on the floor beside her.

CLYDE to BONNIE : *Ohhh! They don't know nothin', do they, honey?*

C.W. has been studying hard on the torn newspaper. Suddenly :

C.W. cheerful and curious : *Hey. How come they always referring to me, the newspapers, as . . . "Un-unidentified sus-suspect?".*

C.W. has trouble with his last phrase. BONNIE laughs. This picks up CLYDE's spirits once more.

CLYDE to C.W. : *You just be glad that's all you are. Long's they don't know your last name.*

MALCOLM toadying to CLYDE, talking to CLARENCE : *That's right, boy. Mr. Barrow's lookin' out for your interests.*

C.W. in the spirit of the thing : *Hey, Pa, how's it feel to have a coupla big deals stayin' in your house, huh?*

MALCOLM friendly as can be : *Ain't that somethin' for me? That's somethin' for me, ain't it?*

CLYDE back in a good mood, expansive : *Uh, you been mighty nice to us. And I want you to let us pay you, say, forty dollars for your hospitality.*

MALCOLM protesting vehemently : *No, no, no. I'm just happy to have you folk here as company. Anybody's a friend of my boy, you know I . . .*

C.W. abruptly : *Hey, Pa, come on, let's go have some supper. I'm starvin'. Come on.*

MALCOLM to CLYDE, as he goes inside : *You're welcome here, you know that.* To BONNIE : *And you just make yourself right at home and stay as long as you want to.*

EXTERIOR MOSS HOUSE KITCHEN

As soon as they are out of earshot from BONNIE and CLYDE, MALCOLM turns on C.W. displaying an entirely different demeanor from the one he presented outside. It is our first clue to MALCOLM's hypocrisy.

MALCOLM indicating the tattoo which shows through C.W.'s open shirt : *You look like trash, all marked up like that. Cheap trash.*

C.W. protesting : *Bonnie says it looks good.*

146

MALCOLM: *What does Bonnie know? She ain't nothing but cheap trash herself. Look what they do to you. You don't ever get your name in the paper! You just get them pictures printed on your skin, by Bonnie and Clyde. Shoot, they ain't nothin' but a coupla kids.*
C.W.: *But, Daddy . . .*
MALCOLM: *I'm so glad your ma ain't alive to see this here thing . . .*
  C.W. peeks at it, peering down at his chest, trying to bring the bluebirds into focus, puzzled.
MALCOLM angrily: *All jellied up like that.*
C.W.: *I don't see what's so, uh, bad about it . . .*
MALCOLM: *You wouldn't!*
  He throws some burning hot batter at C.W.'s chest. C.W. doubles up in pain.

INTERIOR HOSPITAL CORRIDOR
The SHERIFF followed by HAMER and a DEPUTY walk down the drab corridor of the hospital toward the room where BLANCHE is. There are three guards sitting outside the room.
SHERIFF: *The word is out that Bonnie an' Clyde are holed up just out of town. And they're fixin' to bust in here and take Blanche out. So . . .*
HAMER: *All two of 'em?*
  HAMER opens the door and goes into the hospital room.

INTERIOR HOSPITAL ROOM
Seated in a soft chair, near the bed is BLANCHE BARROW. The top of her head, her eyes and nose are completely swathed in bandages. She wears a hospital gown. The room is white and bright. HAMER is in the doorway. He jerks a thumb for the policeman to leave. Quietly, almost on tiptoes, HAMER walks over to BLANCHE. He gets inches away from her face, leaning over her shoulder. She puts a hand up to her ear, trying to discover who is there. Suddenly:
HAMER: *Blanche Barrow.*
  BLANCHE screams, startled. She gropes around her. She is a bit panicked but adjusts to his presence. BLANCHE is now a defeated human being. Her voice and manner bespeak great

sorrow and still a touch of her old high-strung hysteria. But most of that is gone now, like everything else that was really vital in her life.

BLANCHE sobbing: *Who is it?*

HAMER: *I guess it's been kind of rough on you, hasn't it? . . .* Choosing his words carefully: *Bein' the daughter of a preacher, like you are. I imagine old Buck wasn't a bad sort, was he?*

BLANCHE: *No, he wasn't.*

HAMER very slowly, carefully: *I reckon Clyde just sort of led him astray didn't he?*

BLANCHE is crying and it obviously hurts.

HAMER is working up to the crucial point of his conversation with BLANCHE.

HAMER: *That's a . . . shame, Blanche. Yes, ma'am. It's a shame. That he led your Buck astray. Clyde, his own brother . . .* Bonnie. Leaning forward: *And that little feller. The one that was with you when you took that Texas Ranger in Missouri.* Patting her shoulder: *He was with you all along, wasn't he?*

BLANCHE hopelessly: *C.W.*

HAMER: *That's right. C.W. . . . I, er, . . . I don't recollect his last name.*

BLANCHE: *Moss. C.W. Moss.*

Triumphant, HAMER mouthes the words silently with her. BLANCHE starts talking slowly, but gradually warms to the subject, and begins to talk and talk, for the sake of airing her troubles.

BLANCHE: *He was there that day we met 'em. I didn't want to go. I didn't want to. An' Buck said we's just goin' on a visit, so we wouldn't do no stealin' or robbin' . . .*

HAMER starts to creep away. He goes to the wire mesh door and closes it, leaving BLANCHE sitting on the white chair.

BLANCHE: *And we went up to Joplin and all of a sudden . . .* Hysteria begins to creep into her voice as she relives it all . . . *All of a sudden they all just started shooting . . .*

Then the outer door closes, blocking her out in mid-sentence.

EXTERIOR CAR IN FRONT OF THE MOSS FARM (DAY)

It is pouring with rain, middle of the afternoon and BONNIE

and CLYDE are sitting inside the car. They have lived so much
in cars that they tend to still spend much of their time in it
rather than in a room. There they are themselves.

INTERIOR CAR
CLYDE is in the front seat reading newspaper clippings. On the
dashboard is a box of ginger-snaps which he eats while he
reads. BONNIE is in the back seat, her legs wrapped in a plaid
blanket, writing poetry. She looks like Elizabeth Barrett
Browning. She has become totally fragile, the essence of herself.
She is writing on a pad. They look domestic.

CLYDE : *What you writin'?*

BONNIE looking up : *I'm writing a poem about us.*

CLYDE this appeals to his ego : *Let me hear it.*

BCNNIE giggles modestly.

CLYDE : *Come on.*

BONNIE : *Just let me finish this line.*

She does so, CLYDE munches a cookie.

BONNIE : *It's called . . . "The Story of Bonnie and Clyde".*

She reads intensely. At the beginning of this montage, the
camera remains on her face. Behind her we see the rain on the
window.

BONNIE reading : *"You've heard the story of Jesse James —*
    Of how he lived and died:
     If you're still in need
     Of something to read
    Here's the story of Bonnie and Clyde."

CLYDE interrupting : *You think if I sent that into the newspapers,
they'd print it?*

BONNIE frowns and shrugs her shoulders.

CLYDE off-screen : *I'm gonna do it.*

BONNIE reading : *"Now Bonnie and Clyde are the Barrow Gang*
    I'm sure you all have read
     How they rob and steal
     And those who squeal
    Are usually found dying or dead.

    They call them cold-hearted killers;
    They say they are heartless and mean;

> But I say this with pride,
> That I once knew Clyde
> When he was honest and upright and clean.
>
> But the laws fooled around,
> Kept taking him down
> And locking him up in a cell,"

Dissolve to:

INTERIOR POLICE STATION

The manuscript is laying on the desk. HAMER picks it up. BONNIE's voice continues on the soundtrack.

BONNIE's voice over:

> "Till he said to me,
> 'I'll never be free
> So I'll meet a few of them in hell.' "

CLOSE-UP OF A NEWSPAPER PAGE

The poem is printed all the way down the length of one column. On the sound track, BONNIE's voice picks up the recitation:

BONNIE's voice over:

> "If a policeman is killed in Dallas,
> And they have no clue or guide;
> If they can't find a fiend,
> They just wipe their slate clean
> And hang it on Bonnie and Clyde."

EXTERIOR FIELD BONNIE AND CLYDE (DAY)

At first we see only the newspaper clipping with the shadow of CLYDE's face down one side. BONNIE continues reading off-screen, but now she reads directly from the newspaper:

BONNIE off-screen:

> "If they try to act like citizens
> And rent them a nice little flat
> About the third night
> They're invited to fight
> By a sub-gun's rat-a-tat-tat."

BONNIE continues reading the poem, as the camera pulls back slightly to show that it is a different day and they are wearing different clothes. They are sitting on the grass with a picnic hamper behind them. As she stops, she has an expectant and somewhat self-satisfied look.

BONNIE continues reading:

> *"Some day they'll go down together;*
> *They'll bury them side by side;*
> *To few it'll be grief —*
> *To the law a relief —*
> *But it's death for Bonnie and Clyde."*

CLOSE-UP OF CLYDE

His eyes are wide, his mouth open, his face shows surprise and delight.

CLYDE in gleeful wonder: *You know what you done there? You told my story. You told my whole story right there.*

Camera widens to take in BONNIE. She is both moved and delighted by his response. CLYDE gets up, grabs the paper and stares at it, It is all starting to come out now — his realization that he has made it, that he is the stuff of legend, that he is

153

an important figure.

CLYDE: *Right there! One time I told you I was gonna make you somebody. That's what you done for me.*

BONNIE giggles.

CLYDE serious: *You made me somebody they're gonna remember.*
He looks at her tenderly and stretches out a hand.

CLOSE-UP   BONNIE
Now laughing too, with a great feeling of joy.

TWO SHOT   BONNIE AND CLYDE
He pulls her to him, his face inches away from hers, about to kiss her. She is waiting, expecting . . . Suddenly, he kisses her. She kisses back. They are locked together. They grow more ardent; they pull back and laugh again. They begin to make love.

EXTERIOR   ARCADIA STREET
ICE CREAM PARLOR   (DAY)
Bright afternoon. Camera is across the street from an ice cream parlor. Sign above it: "EVA'S HAND-PACKED ICE CREAM". A large plate glass window fronts the store, and through it we can see the people inside seated at tables and booth. Prominent in our vision is MALCOLM MOSS, seated, facing camera. He is seated across from another man, but we see him from the back. MALCOLM is obviously doing a lot of talking and then some hard listening; gesticulating and looking disturbed. After a bit of this, he rises from the table and begins walking toward the door. The other man rises and turns. We now see that it is FRANK HAMER. MALCOLM and HAMER come out onto the sidewalk, squinting in the sunlight. MALCOLM mimes some social pleasantries by way of saying "goodbye", but HAMER'S face shows no emotion or recognition of the gesture. He turns and walks away, walking out of the frame. MALCOLM stands where he is, in front of the ice cream parlor. By the expression on his face, we can see that he is rather disturbed by what he has heard and that he is still grappling with the problem.

154

EXTERIOR FIELD   BONNIE AND CLYDE
(LATE AFTERNOON)
They lie where they were with one difference — they are now
wrapped in the blanket. CLYDE sits up, his shirt undone to the
waist. He casts a sidelong glance to BONNIE, wanting some sort
of overt reaction from her. She's just smiling slightly. CLYDE's
underlying anxiety begins to surface.
CLYDE not looking at her : *H'h. Hey, eh, how do you feel?*
BONNIE watching him steadily, her slight smile growing : *Fine.*
CLYDE anxious : *I mean, you feel the way you're s'posed to feel
when you're, when you're . . . After you're . . .*
BONNIE : *Yeah, just.*
CLYDE doesn't know what the fuck to say, desperately wants her
approval : *M'hm. Well, that's . . . that's good, isn't it? Look I—I
figure that it's a good idea to ask, because how else you gonna
know if it . . . You know . . .*
BONNIE stopping him with great warmth: *Hey. You did just perfect.*
    CLYDE looks at her for the first time, tremendously relieved.
    He can see she means it. Now his buoyancy, utterly unchained,
    breaks through :
CLYDE : *I did, didn't I? I mean I really did. I never figured on
that. Damm!*
    Lovingly, laughing, altogether overwhelmed with himself,
    CLYDE pulls BONNIE into him. He kisses her, wants to make
    love again, but then pulls back and keeps chattering sixty
    miles a minute. He's waited twenty-three years to talk about
    this, and he's got the perfect audience.

INTERIOR   KITCHEN   MOSS FARM
It is after dinner. There are four empty plates, but only C.W.
and MALCOLM in the kitchen. C.W. is scraping the bottom of
a wilted " EVA'S HAND-PACKED ICE CREAM " carton.
MALCOLM studies his son's quiet intensity in this direction for
a moment, then moves very close, whispers when he speaks.
MALCOLM whispering : *Boy, did they expect you to go downtown
with 'em tomorrow?*
C.W. out loud, licking his ice cream : *Who?*
MALCOLM raising his own voice, infuriated by his son's obtuseness:
Bonnie and Clyde! . . . that's who. He slaps the carton out of

155

C.W.'s hands whispering again: *Bonnie and Clyde.*

C.W. unconcerned: *Sure, always go with 'em.*

MALCOLM thinks hard about this.

MALCOLM: *Yeah, you better, you better go. But when they go to get in their car to come on home, don't you get back in there with 'em.*

C.W. genuinely puzzled: *Why, Daddy?*

MALCOLM: *You listen to your Pa for once! Cain't you do that? I'm your Pa, I'm your kin. Not that there Clyde Barrow.*

C.W. still confused: *What you want me to tell 'em? "I can't get back in the car with you?"*

MALCOLM is ready to kill — his son's obtuseness and his fear of CLYDE is whipping him into quiet frenzy.

MALCOLM squeezing C.W.'s arm: *You tell 'em nothin', you hear?* He hesitates, then: *I made a deal and got you off with a coupla years!*

MALCOLM hauls off and whacks C.W. across the top of his head with the flat of his hand, then momentarily holds his hand over C.W.'s mouth.

MALCOLM, we can see his own fear: *You just be sure that you're off the streets in that town when they go to get in their car.*

C.W. suddenly smiles, as if he knew something.

C.W. expletive: *You think . . . laws is gonna catch Bonnie and Clyde in town?*

C.W. returns to the ice cream carton . . .

MALCOLM lets him, figuring he better find out what he can.

C.W. matter of fact: *Clyde's got a sense. Don't you know, Daddy? Nobody catches Clyde. Never . . . Never.*

MALCOLM knows better, but for a moment he stares at his son, fearing that maybe C.W., for all his limitations, has a sense about CLYDE's sense. C.W. has finished with the carton and crumples it, licking the last remnants of cream off his fingers.

INTERIOR BEDROOM MOSS FARM (NIGHT)

BONNIE and CLYDE's bedroom. Both are sitting up in bed, laughing.

BONNIE in a voice charged with anticipation and dream: *What would you do, what would you do if some miracle happened . . .*

156

and we could walk out of here tomorrow morning and start all over again. Clean. With no record and nobody after us? H'm?

CLYDE thinks about it a minute.

CLYDE : *Well, eh, I—I guess I'd do it all different. First off, I wouldn't live in the same state where we pull our jobs. We'd live in a, in another state, and stay clean there. And then when we wanted to take a bank, we'd go into the other state.*

It is the worst thing he could have said, it was not the answer BONNIE wanted to hear. He looks down at her, his voice anxious.

CLYDIE : *Bonnie?*

She is silent.

CLYDE : *Bonnie . . .*

But she does not answer. She smiles slightly and sadly.

EXTERIOR   ARCADIA STREET

A street in Arcadia. The car is parked. BONNIE and CLYDE walk toward it carrying big bags of groceries and supplies and put them inside. CLYDE opens the door for BONNIE then gets into the driving seat and takes off his shoes.

CLYDE looking around : *What happened to C. W.?*

BONNIE : *Oh, he's over there in the hardware store, getting some light bulbs for his daddy.*

INTERIOR   CAR   ARCADIA STREET

CLYDE reaches in his shirt pocket and takes out his sunglasses. As he goes to put them on, one of the lenses falls out,

CLYDE : *Whoops!*

He puts them on.

BONNIE laughing : *You gonna wear 'em like that?*

CLYDE : *Drive with one eye closed.*

BONNIE rummages around in one of the bags and pulls out something wrapped in tissue paper. She unwraps it and puts it on the dashboard, displaying it.

CLOSE-UP   STATUETTE

It is a little porcelain shepherdess holding a crook in her hand, worth about thirty cents.

157

CLYDE pointing at the ice cream parlor nearby: *Want some ice cream?*

BONNIE admiring the shepherdess: *No! Look here. Isn't that just the prettiest thing you ever saw? Look, you see, you can see every fingernail of her hand.*

She shows him.

CLYDE: *That's the prettiest thing. Hey, where is that boy?*

EXTERIOR   HARDWARE STORE
A couple of men sit idly outside the hardware store. C.W. is nowhere to be seen.

INTERIOR   CAR
BONNIE: *Oh, listen, I'll go get him, okay?*
She gets out and CLYDE closes the door.

EXTERIOR   ARCADIA STREET
A couple of deputies drive past in a Sheriff's Department automobile.

INTERIOR STORE CLOSE-UP C.W.
C.W. hiding inside a store, peering out through a curtained window. His expression is disturbed, his face half in shadow.

EXTERIOR STREET
The Sheriff's Department automobile drives up and parks next to CLYDE. CLYDE, hiding his face, closes his door and starts the car as one of the Deputies gets out, acknowledging him with a wave. CLYDE backs the car hurriedly out into the road and pulls up outside the hardware store, calling out to BONNIE who is talking cheerfully to a little girl.

CLYDE: *Gladys Jean.*

BONNIE is puzzled.

CLYDE: *Time to go home now.*

BONNIE thinks it is a joke. But CLYDE jerks his head back in the direction of the deputies. She understands. Licking her lips, she saunters forward and gets quickly into the car. It drives off round the corner, not too fast and not too slow.

INTERIOR STORE CLOSE-UP C.W.
C.W. smiles with relief.

EXTERIOR   ROADSIDE

We see MALCOLM jacking up the back wheel of his pick-up truck which is parked on the side of the road in a wooded area.

INTERIOR   CAR

BONNIE and CLYDE are keyed up after their narrow escape in town. CLYDE tweaks BONNIE'S nose.

CLYDE : *Get back there in about twenty minutes and we'll pick him up. I tell you, if that boy didn't have his head strapped on him, he'd lose it!*

BONNIE burrows in a grocery bag and comes out with a pear. She takes a big bite. The juice drips down the side of her mouth. She looks beautiful. She holds it out for him, and he takes a bite. They are relaxed, confident again.

EXTERIOR   ROAD   (DAY)

BONNIE and CLYDE's car coming down the road.

BONNIE : *Hey, isn't that Malcolm there?*

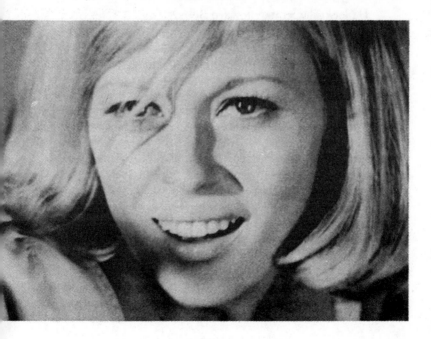

CAMERA sees from CLYDE's point of view MALCOLM standing in the road, waving him down. The pickup truck, its back jacked up, is parked beside him on a shoulder of the road.

EXTERIOR   ROAD

CLYDE reaches the spot, pulls off the road and stops the car. He gets out, still munching the pear. BONNIE stays in the car, watching through the windscreen.

CLYDE : *What you got there?*

MALCOLM : *Got a flat tire. Ain't got no spare.*

Suddenly a truck loaded with chickens comes riding down the road from the opposite direction.

EXTERIOR   NEW ANGLE

A flock of birds flies out from the trees. The sound of their wing-beats is a little like gunfire.

The old man suddenly dives under his truck to hide.

CLYDE : *Hey* . . . His smile suddenly fades.

CLOSE-UP   CLYDE

He looks desperately toward BONNIE.

CLOSE-UP   BONNIE

Tearful and loving, she returns his last look.

EXTERIOR   ROADSIDE

Hidden in the undergrowth, HAMER has seen the chicken truck from a long way away and realises he cannot afford to let anything pass between him and his quarry. He decides the time is now. The shooting starts.

We see the chicken truck. Two men in the front seat. They see ahead of them an incredible shooting match, and, in terror, they jam on the brakes. The noise is rapid, deafening. In all, the laws fire eighty-seven shots into BONNIE and CLYDE, giving them absolutely no chance.

We see, alternately, the bodies of CLYDE and BONNIE twisting, shaking, horribly distorted; much of the action is in slow motion. CLYDE is on the ground, his body arching and rolling from the impact of the bullets. BONNIE is still in her seat : her body jerking and swaying as the bullets thud relentlessly

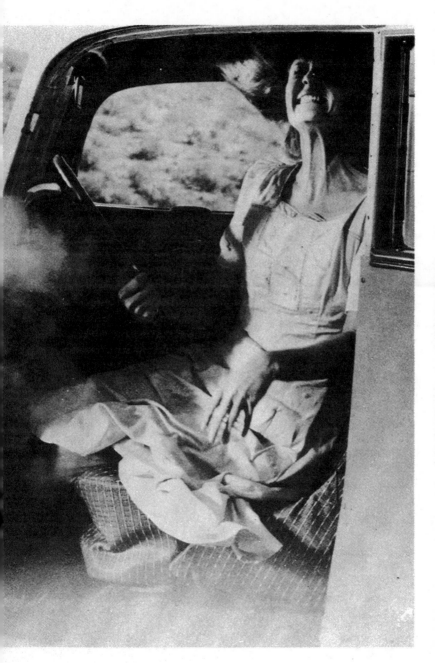

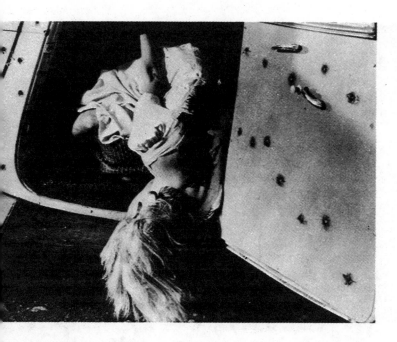

into her and the framework of the car.

EXTERIOR THE CAR ON THE VERGE

BONNIE's body slews out sideways, head first. A final burst and her head and shoulders drop down on to the running board. CLYDE's body rolls over and over on the ground and then lies still. The firing stops.

Utter silence. It has been a massacre. BONNIE and CLYDE never had a chance to return the gunfire.

EXTERIOR ROADSIDE

A pause. MALCOLM begins to crawl out from under his truck and the men in the chicken truck jump down. Slowly, from out of the undergrowth on the other side of the road, the six lawmen emerge. On the faces of the five deputies, horror and shock at what they have just done. HAMER, however, registers no emotions. His face is a blank. Slowly, slowly, the men begin to edge closer to the car to see the result. MALCOLM and the chicken farmers join them. The group of men stare silently down at the bodies of BONNIE and CLYDE.

André Labarthe and Jean-Louis Comolli

THE ARTHUR PENN INTERVIEW

CAHIERS DU CINEMA : *In comparison with* Bonnie and Clyde *and* The Left-Handed Gun, *the scenario of* The Chase *seems less worked over, sometimes even clumsy. The first sequence of the film, for example, hardly seems to integrate with the rest. What sort of importance do you attach to your work on the actual scenario of a film?*

ARTHUR PENN : The basic story for *The Left-Handed Gun* was very simple. My main problem was to fill it out first by developing Billy's relationships with his friends (especially the Scot), then, along with the scriptwriter, Leslie Stevens, by systematically going over all the other aspects of the film. The scenario of *Bonnie and Clyde* was already very complete, very fully written up, from the beginning. It was not, incidentally, entirely uninfluenced by Truffaut. However, I asked the scriptwriters to work on it with me, as I usually do, and to make a number of changes in it, which they accepted. And in fact, they integrated my ideas in their script so well that, as with *The Left-Handed Gun,* the collaboration between myself and the scriptwriters was quite real. And that is just what didn't happen with *The Chase.*

CAHIERS : *Why couldn't you collaborate with Lillian Hellman as you do with other scriptwriters?*

PENN : The producer, Sam Spiegel, got someone else to rewrite what she'd done. And so the situation just became totally confused : one day we had a piece of script by Lillian Hellman, another day something by Horton Foote, then a piece reworked by Ivan Moffet and sometimes, I reckon, a few passages by Sam Spiegel himself. That was a mess !

CAHIERS : *Brando gives an extraordinary performance in the scene where he gets beaten up. He really looks as though he is being hit and the effect of violence is much greater . . .*

PENN : Brando himself had a number of ideas for the beating-up scene. First we filmed the fight normally, then we shot it at a higher speed, at 16 frames, then Brando really did hit his opponents and got himself hit too.

CAHIERS : *Let's turn to* Mickey One . . .

PENN: The film was shot in Chicago, after a special agreement with Columbia, who were producing it. The Columbia management gave me all the money I needed and didn't interfere at all in the film. It was in fact written into the contract that they hadn't even the right to read the scenario. It should really have been a better film, because I was left totally free with it.

CAHIERS: *With* The Chase, *though, you seem to have been hindered by the workings of the Hollywood machine . . .*

PENN: That's true. It was terrible making a film with so many technicians around, so many very experienced, very able people. If you have an idea, it immediately gets filtered down, like smoke in a filter cigarette. All the people round you think they know exactly how your idea should be presented, but what finally comes out of all their very precise efforts is not your idea at all, but the archetypal, commonplace, banal Hollywood idea. And if you want to avoid that, you've got to say no to the people working round you all the time. You've got to refuse systematically everything they propose, from a slight difference in colour to the choice of a necktie. If you want the final outcome of your work to be totally yours, to express you personally, then you've got to watch everything in every sequence, to be absolutely sure that the slightest detail is exactly as you want it. But obviously, it isn't long before you have neither the interest, and certainly not the energy, to do everything yourself. And that's why, finally, *The Chase* became a film by Hollywood rather than a film by Penn.

CAHIERS: *In* Mickey One *and* Bonnie and Clyde, *you have made two films with Warren Beatty. How do you work with him? Does he collaborate with you on the scenario or on the conception of the characters?*

PENN: As far as *Mickey One* was concerned, no. In the case of *Bonnie and Clyde,* Warren Beatty not only produced the film but also bought the scenario. And there we did discuss all the problems together, and he did have some say in the final rewriting of the scenario. The only really important change came in the role of Bonnie, and this was suggested by Faye Dunaway herself. She thought that, towards the end of the film, Bonnie and Clyde should finally get round to making love. She spoke to me about it and I agreed with her. I spoke to Warren, who'd had the same idea himself, and so we adopted it. As an actor, Warren took his role

166

very seriously, and played it exactly as I asked him. I know he has the reputation of being a very difficult young man to direct, but we got on very well together and we talk to each other in a way which seems to get round problems: very basic, very direct and very natural.

CAHIERS: *After* Mickey One, *didn't some small difference occur between you?*

PENN: Yes. Our relationship was difficult. Warren didn't want to play the part as I wanted him to, because he just didn't see it in the same way. And we didn't really get a very good understanding between us. But before beginning *Bonnie and Clyde,* we made an agreement to tell each other very frankly what we thought of each other, violently if necessary. We also agreed that, in the case of total disagreement, it would be he who would give way and do what I wanted. As it turned out, curiously enough, we had the same ideas. The only point on which we did disagree for a time was the choice of Faye Dunaway for Bonnie. At the beginning, he didn't like her, and thought she wasn't what we needed for Bonnie. But after working with her, he realised about half-way through the shooting that she was perfect.

CAHIERS: *Was the shooting chronological?*

PENN: No. I wanted it to be, but it wasn't possible.

CAHIERS: *Because we have the same reaction as Beatty towards Dunaway; we don't like her at the beginning, but later . . .*

PENN: We deliberately set out to produce this evolution in the spectator's attitude towards Faye Dunaway. At the beginning of the film she had to appear rather vulgar, in no way charming or likeable, so that, after the first love scene with Clyde, when it becomes evident that he's impotent, we can appreciate that she is moved, touched by this weakness, and that, from then on, Bonnie's personality changes.

CAHIERS: *It is possible to see certain similarities between the leading character of* The Left-Handed Gun *and Clyde. For both of them, life is a game which they play with a revolver, like children. And both of them die, but only after they have undergone a sort of metamorphosis, after they have changed. Could it be said that, for you, the hero of* The Left-Handed Gun *was also impotent?*

PENN: I don't think so. He was young, infantile even, and the only woman he slept with was his old friend's wife. He just wasn't interested in having an affair and you could even say he had certain elements of an Oedipus complex. He wasn't exactly impotent, though he might have been almost.

CAHIERS : *In* Bonnie and Clyde *you carry to the extreme a tendency to juxtapose sequences which explore the violence of various situations to their fullest* . . .

PENN : I wanted the film to have a certain rhythm, a nervous montage. Also, my memory of Bonnie and Clyde was from snapshots; I didn't want a moving camera that would stay on a scene for a long time. I wanted something more kaleidoscopic.

CAHIERS : *Each shot in your film seems to serve a dual purpose: it carries forward the film's story and it also adds a new piece of information to what went on before, with a technique which makes each sequence almost autonomous* . . .

PENN : It is in the service of the notion of irony. Very often we would lead the audience to believe one thing, and then in the next sequence we turn around. For example, in the beginning of the film, at the abandoned farm, when the farmer says that the bank took his house away : at that point Bonnie and Clyde know they're robbers, but they don't know what they want to rob. They know that they're outlaws, but for what? At the end of that sequence we have a close-up of Warren saying, "We rob banks." It's an afterthought; he discovers afterwards what he was doing earlier. We are dealing with a sort of primitive intellect. Clyde is not a very intelligent or complicated man, but a man full of desire to act. He must act but he doesn't know why. In this film, that was what we meant by "doing". Socially, the people were paralysed by the Depression; for example, the scene in the camp near the end is nearly stylized in its immobility. I was trying to say that everybody else was still—frozen by the atmosphere, by the Depression. At least Bonnie and Clyde were mobile and functioning —sometimes on behalf of foolish things, sometimes self-destructively —but at least they functioned.

CAHIERS : *What did you ask Faye Dunaway to do for the last sequence of the film, when she looks through the car window?*

PENN : I told her : "Look at Clyde"—in the direction where Warren was supposed to be. At the last moment, though, I made Warren move to one side and put myself there instead, so that she has this sweet, kind look and, although she finally broke the effect by looking surprised, I kept this look, because that's what I wanted and what I'd been looking for.

CAHIERS : *When I saw you working in Hollywood, I was struck by the fact that you speak very quietly to your actors, though most other directors shout a lot . . .*

PENN : Sometimes I just do it to make them feel relaxed or more confident, but sometimes there is another reason for it. For instance, I might want to tell them something about the character of another actor, something which the other doesn't know. So, when shooting starts, the one who isn't in on the secret wonders : "What's Penn been saying to him? What's he asked him to do?" And I think this adds tension, a sort of liveliness, to a scene ; you even get a sort of anxiety in the actors' looks which gives something more to a sequence, fills out its interest. Sometimes, though, what I say has nothing to do directly or indirectly with the shooting. It could be : "Do you want a cigarette, or go to the washroom?" Little things like that, which make people feel they can start working like human beings again and not like machines . . .

CAHIERS : *Just when Clyde dies there's a shot from above—he turns, we see him from behind, his body rises like a wave, and then the shot changes. Was that a preconceived idea or did you get it as you were shooting?*

PENN : I had the idea before I started shooting. I wanted to get the spasm of death, and so I used four cameras, each one at a different speed, 24, 48, 72 and 96, I think, and different lenses, so that I could cut to get the shock and at the same time the ballet of death. There's a moment in death when the body no longer functions, when it becomes an object and has a certain kind of detached ugly beauty. It was that aspect I was trying to get.

CAHIERS : *What about Bonnie's death?*

PENN : I wanted two kinds of death : Clyde's to be rather like a ballet, and Bonnie's to have the physical shock. So we shot it with all those different cameras. We put on the bullet holes—and there's even a piece of Warren's head that comes off, like that famous photograph of Kennedy.

CAHIERS : *What did you ask the actress to do at that point?*

PENN : Just to be, simply to enact the death, to fall and follow the laws of gravity. Faye was trapped behind the wheel. We tied one leg to the gear shift so that she would feel free to fall, but wouldn't fall out of the car. We shot it three or four times to get this feeling, and changed speed and lenses constantly to get this sort of change of pace in space and time.

CAHIERS : *And this also creates an aura of unreality about Clyde's death . . .*

PENN : Yes, because I knew it would be the end of the film. We could have done a killing which would be very gross and vulgar— really obscene and terribly ugly—where you see him simply torn apart, but that didn't seem to me to be an accurate end, because the death of these two people is a foregone conclusion. It's not as if it just happened. Since you know it's going to happen, I figure you should do an abstraction of it rather than a replica of it.

CAHIERS : *This introduces an almost mythic element in the final part of the film . . .*

PENN : Exactly. Which is equally true for *The Left-Handed Gun,* but, alas, the present end has been added on, and it's clearly not mine. When Billy falls, there was a little procession through the village, women with candles, who draw round Billy's body and sit down close to him . . . just a small ritual to close the cycle of the legend. Then someone added that idiotic ending with the Sheriff's wife saying "You can go back home now," which just doesn't make sense.

CAHIERS : *Wouldn't it have been preferable to end* Bonnie and Clyde *with the shot of Beatty turning, rather than shots of the posse coming out and surrounding the car?*

PENN : We tried that and it seemed too abrupt, and because it was so abrupt it became almost self-conscious. It gave me the feeling of not having those last few notes of a symphony. You know that this is the end but you need the last three or four notes just to finish it, for form only, because it's over as far as content. The moment he rolls over, the moment her hand stops, that was the end of the story. To end there seemed to change the meaning, to take away from its faintly abstract quality. It seemed like we were trying to do a replica, brutal and severe; we wanted a mythical, legendary, balletic ending.

CAHIERS : *Did you ever conceive of the construction of your film in terms of one or more musical forms?*

PENN : The two young journalists who wrote the script had interviewed Flatt and Scruggs in Nashville, Tennessee, and suggested we use the five-string country banjo. That gave us an idea of what kind of music to use. We used Flatt and Scruggs and a young composer who wrote some other music in the same spirit.

CAHIERS : *In the beginning of* Bonnie and Clyde *the tone is one of burlesque and then becomes pathetic. Did this shift exist in the scenario itself?*

PENN : Yes. It started as a chronicle of some amusing kids who dug up these funny things to do—a little bit outside the law but not too serious. The way we set up the first killing—they can't get the car out, the man jumps on the running board of the car, and they shoot him right in the face—it's to come right out of laughter. The idea was for us to be laughing and suddenly it was just to happen —"I killed somebody, I didn't mean to do that, I was just robbing a bank, I didn't . . ."—it was to have that kind of innocence.

CAHIERS : *All deaths are extremely distressing and very bloody . . .*

PENN : Very bloody and very painful. My own experience—it's not very broad—is that blood always surprises me, the amount of blood—too much. It recalls Shakespeare's line, "Who would have thought the old man to have had so much blood in him?" In film, when you show a death, it should have that shock effect. But at the end of *Bonnie and Clyde,* we didn't do the same kind of death ; we were trying to change the character of death, to make their deaths more legendary than real.

CAHIERS : *Is it in order to arouse conflicting feelings in the public that you utilize these constant shifts in tone?*

PENN : In *Bonnie and Clyde,* we don't have a story of very strong characters. They're relatively shallow, rather empty people as far as we know. Nice enough, and with certain problems, but we don't have a moral dilemma which would help us to understand what the characters are going through in their interior lives. Consequently, we had to deal more at the level of the outer side, like the cartoon, more the outline. I thought in terms of cartoons—each frame changing. Here we laugh, here we cry, here we laugh again, and so we cut the film like that and the images were made up like that instead of long, fluid ones.

CAHIERS : *Which gives* Bonnie and Clyde *a painful dimension.*

PENN : Absolutely, though this wasn't so in my other films, *The Left-Handed Gun* or *Mickey One,* for example. I was interested there in the thoughts of the characters, and their motives, especially if they were illogical. The characters in this film, though, are killers and gangsters, people who seem barely conscious of what they are doing. I couldn't give them a deep inner life they hadn't got. Which doesn't mean that I wanted to make them in any way inconsistent, or make them body-less, shallow, theoretical creatures. I hope that some sense of their real existence comes over, even if the rather cool tone of the story takes precedence over psychological analysis.

CAHIERS : *But doesn't it seem dangerous to you to be able to manipulate at will the reactions of the public which, being less interested in the characters, is only responsive to your manipulation?*

PENN : Yes, it seems to me a little dangerous, but it seemed to be the best way to tell this story. We have to begin with the fact that these two people were killers; they were gangsters; they seemed to have almost no conscience. Since I couldn't find a deep interior life for them, I decided really to stay outside, to change as swiftly as I could from one sentiment to another. I hope that a certain kind of life comes out of that, but, in point of fact, you know very little of what they really were feeling or thinking because it's more of a chronicle than the story of any one person's struggle with his time. We used laughter to get the audience to feel like a member of the gang, to have the feeling of adventure, a feeling of playing together. Then, near the end of the film, we begin to turn a little bit. The humour fades when Bonnie says she wants to see her mother. When the mother says to her, "You try to live three miles from me and you won't live long, honey", the humour in the film really ends. We hope by then that you're already trapped, that you're caught in the film as a member of the gang and now you have to go along. Bonnie's and Clyde's deaths really begin at that point and from there on it's waiting out history.

CAHIERS : *What are your plans for future films?*

PENN : I'm working on one about an American Indian.* Again, it's a comic story, but we'll have scenes that will be as terrible as the lot of the American Indian really is—and really was in Custer's time. Of course, the analogy is with the American Negro, but at the moment at least, I don't know how to do a film about the American Negro that wouldn't be a distortion or a romance, or

---

Little Big Man (1970)

172

too limited in its views. But if I could approach the problem by way of an analogy, then I could express myself better. Anyway, I'm only at the planning stage yet.

CAHIERS : *Can you explain to us the kind of problems you would encounter in making a film about negroes?*

PENN : I have to have perspective. I don't have a view sufficiently complete to be able to know how to make a film about it. I can tell lots of incidents that would be terrible and unpleasant and show injustice, but they wouldn't be saying anything because I don't know the end. Making a film about the Indians might help me to understand that. It's very interesting that during a screening of *Bonnie and Clyde* one evening, five negroes present there completely identified with Bonnie and Clyde. They were delighted. They said : "This is the way; that's the way to go, baby. Those cats were all right". They really understood, because in a certain sense the American negro has the same kind of attitude of "I have nothing more to lose", that was true during the Depression for Bonnie and Clyde. It is true now of the American negro. He is really at the point of revolution—it's rebellion, not riot.

CAHIERS : *Are you still carrying on with your work in the theatre?*

PENN : The situation has changed a lot in the United States. There was a time when you worked seriously in the theater and you went off to Hollywood, that you had to prostitute yourself more or less. Now the opposite is true. You can do more serious, more truthful things in the cinema. There's nothing worth while done on Broadway now, everything's intended as pure amusement.

CAHIERS : *What about off-Broadway?*

PENN : It's the same as on-Broadway. It's just as expensive, and you have the same limited audience, bourgeois, white, from a certain social level, very satisfied with itself, and which wouldn't want to see its habits of thought changed for anything in the world. You can still do serious work, though, in the off-off-Broadway theaters. In the Massachusetts theater, for instance, we've started putting on new plays which are much nearer to the cinema in theme and technique . . . I work on Broadway to make a living, but I really live in the little Stockbridge theater, which satisfies more my idea about what theater should be.

(This interview first appeared in Cahiers du Cinéma, December 1967. Reproduced by permission.)

Robert Towne

A TRIP WITH BONNIE AND CLYDE

The time was 1966. *Bonnie and Clyde* was to be filmed in Texas, where the story of Bonnie Parker and Clyde Barrow began, where so much of it took place, and so much of it remains—in the memory of those who lived through the hard times thirty-three years ago, and in the rutted roads and clap-board towns just outside of Dallas. These towns are virtually unchanged since the Depression. They lie scattered about like dusty dominoes on the oppressive, table-flat lands surrounding Big D. They bear handles like Pilots Point and Midlothian and Ponder, names that harken back to old Anglo-Saxon origins, ageless names for towns that indeed, seem to exist outside of time.

Of Texas weather it's been said, "If you don't like it, wait a minute." Battalions of black clouds, blazing sun, sheets of rain, and a whipping wind are liable to pass over, on, and through you in the course of a day. Film making in a capricious climate is a little like making love to a woman whose husband is known to have a violent temper. At least the same question must be asked—considering the risk, is it going to be all that much better? Why not just bed down on the Universal back lot? It's more comfortable and there's less chance of being caught with your pants down.

Two things were striking about the first shot of the Midlothian street down which Bonnie and Clyde walked, and not until the dailies. First, the realization that high tension wires and telephone poles never seem to show up on back lots, but that when you look at a small town, they are a *constant*. They provide perspective when they line the road and sky, giving a hint of the town's size, and most importantly, they're something the eye is accustomed to half-seeing. They make things real and they are missed more by their absence than remarked on by their presence. "It's a war against unreality," Warren had said one day. Without things like crab grass, telephone poles, pimples, poorly patched asphalt in the streets—you've got a back lot and you've already begun to lose your battle with all the artificial elements you fight against in trying to make what appears on film look real, or credible. . . .

There was another kind of climate in Dallas, one as inescapable

174

as the weather. Almost all the city's residents who lived in the days of Bonnie and Clyde remember them and what it was like to read about them almost daily, in the papers.

During those Dust Bowl days, "you was doin' well to get yourself a rabbit," Duryl Barrow, Clyde's now thirty-nine year old nephew said one day on the set. You might go to bed hungry, and defeated, but come morning the paper would bring its daily tales of "the phantom of the Southwest and his yellow haired companion" in another of their daring escapes from "the laws".

Now all these residents—those who actually knew them as well as read about them, went to school with them, worked with them, were robbed by them, not robbed by them, tried to catch them, were neighbours of their sorely tried parents—flocked to the "sets", which often meant that they walked out of the front door of the house they lived in. They all wanted "to see Bonnie and Clyde agin."

It was as if these two were distant, killin' cousins to all of central Texas. Even children of grammar school age today in Dallas know all about Bonnie and Clyde. Bob Benton and David Newman, who were born about the time Clyde and Bonnie died, had written the original screenplay. Benton had grown up in a small Texas town, and had been constantly fed on wild tales of the two "fugitives from justice", as the papers called them in the style of the day. Hearst headlines had made Bonnie Parker and Clyde Barrow escapist entertainment throughout the entire country, but as the people came to the set to look and to almost compulsively tell what they knew about them, it became clear that in Texas they meant more to the people than entertainment. In Texas Bonnie and Clyde were legend.

Furthermore, relatively large numbers of people break heads and laws, even, you might say *especially* even, in Texas. Few of them become folk heroes in the process. All of us, I believe, found ourselves listening for the origins of their legend even as we continued to shoot scenes already committed to paper. What was it about them that made the people of those towns and that time make more of them than they were? Would it come into focus on film?

Arthur, waiting on a light change during the shooting of the abandoned farm sequence, would lean on a rickety fence, still holding the cigar that he continually waved over the entire pro-

175

ceedings like a magic wand, and listen. Warren, when off the set and off the phones, would wander sometimes among the spectators with their stark, staring Walker Evans' faces, listening as they would tell him about who he really was, in their flat, grave twangs. The crew, hanging around the lunch truck or the honey wagon, would swap the newest stories *they'd* heard about Bonnie and Clyde, as though it were from *that* morning's paper, or the freshest kind of gossip.

"Bonnie? You hear she was pregnant when they shot her up in Louisiana? . . . Pregnant? . . . I heard she was *crowning.*" . . . "Nossir. There weren't no Texas Rangers on that job up in Louisiana. We don't play that way . . ." (To this day the Texas laws seem inclined to dissociate themselves from that final brutal ambush in Louisiana.) "They wasn't bad . . . they just got into trouble and had to keep runnin' . . . that was it . . ." ". . . oh, sure, Clyde and Bonnie, they knew they was gonna get it . . . they'd already gone to the undertakers and paid for their funerals" ". . . folks was for 'em for quite a while . . . down in Duncan-ville they robbed one bank five times. Nobody liked that banker much anyways . . . farmers down there'd let Bonnie and Clyde come on their place and keep the laws off of 'em with shotguns . . . they weren't mean, once they started it, they just had to keep goin'." "Bonnie?—shiiiit, she didn't smoke cigars. That was just a joke." "When they was killed, there was this big parade on the West Dallas Road. Thousands of people came out to watch 'em bring their bodies home . . . I was about seventeen then. I wrote a poem about it . . ."

. . . With this continuing body of legend surrounding the shooting, it began to seem sometimes that the process of film-making was being reversed. Life was shaping art. Warren and Faye were not working on Bonnie and Clyde; Bonnie and Clyde were working on them. They were seeping into the actors, with them always, a pervasive and subtle part of the location, along with the high tension wires and domino towns and rutted roads, but as continuing and inescapable as the weather . . .

J. Edgar Hoover and Hearst had dubbed them "the Bloody Barrows", had made them out to be brutal and brilliant bank robbers who killed and made one big killing after another. Killers, they were, about fourteen times, in fact. But if they were bloody,

176

they never killed in cold blood—it was inevitably in the course of flight from a robbery or just flight from pursuit. There was nothing gratuitous about it. And, they were only so-so as bank robbers. They never really tried for a big take, and certainly never succeeded. Like most desperadoes and unlike most syndicate gangsters, Clyde had no head for big business. In practice, the way it worked out was that the vaunted Barrow Gang robbed barely enough to finance their flight from the robberies they committed.

Extracts from an article by Robert Towne which first appeared in Cinema *(U.S.) Vol. 3, No. 5. Reproduced by permission*

WARREN BEATTY AS PRODUCER

CURTIS LEE HANSON: *Would you mind if we discussed your role as producer rather than an actor in* Bonnie and Clyde?

WARREN BEATTY: I would *rather*. Acting is difficult to talk about anyway. It's easier to talk about something that's not so important to you. I don't think I'll produce often.

HANSON: *Were you attracted to* Bonnie and Clyde *originally by the relationship between the two characters?*

BEATTY: The particular relationship between them interests me less than the relationship of the two of them to their society and the times. The Freudian nature of their own relationship puts me to sleep. I've seen too much of that. I'm more interested in the kind of pathetic things that they did. The absolute non-existence of any regard for their society. The public's treatment of them. The love/hate that the public felt for them. The desperation for the little guy to get out of the crowd. That interests me. Clyde wanted to be somebody.

HANSON: *How did you come to produce the picture?*

BEATTY: In the beginning, I did not want to produce. It was the result of doing all the various things that a producer would normally do. In fact, up until the very last minute, I had intended to call in an outsider to actually produce the picture, because the studio said it would be too much work. But I changed my mind. All those things that used to be reserved for someone who felt a responsibility for the quality of the picture, today seem to be spread out in so many different departments that everybody has a cop-out for the failure of the project. I found, in other pictures that I have done, some trivial, some not, an awful lot of people were saying to me, "What the hell do you think you are? A producer?" So . . .

HANSON: *How do you find dealing with actors now that you are in the role of producer?*

BEATTY: I was influenced by a few directors, a few producers, and studio men, and agents, and so on, to have a certain contempt for my own craft in the beginning. The further I go, the more respect I get for the craft of acting, and the greater affection I have for

178

actors. The more intelligent an actor is, the more inventive and the more creative he is. I am very happy to say, I like actors the best. The narcissism of an actor cannot even begin to be compared to the narcissism of a writer. And the megalomania of a movie director is something to scratch your head about. These are things that nearly everyone attacks actors for . . .

Making a movie, no matter how you slice it, is the work of a committee. There has to be a boss of the committee, but there are other elements besides the boss. A healthy situation in movie making is when a certain amount of hostile intelligence can be directed against another hostile intelligence in an amiable atmosphere that doesn't deter either intelligence from functioning well. I am just beginning to climb out of this cavalcade of crap that says, "Just do what the director says. Do anything he tells you." Of course, it *can* work that way but it is not the healthiest atmosphere possible. Kazan would never put you in that position. Kazan would get mad if you didn't tell what you really felt about a scene. He would feel that you were depriving him of his right as a co-worker. He would eventually do it the way he felt, which is correct. There must be a boss to a committee, and the creative boss in movies is the director.
HANSON : *Certain successful directors don't like to work creatively with a committee.*
BEATTY : True. And if they don't like to, they shouldn't. Basically, success breeds intolerance to the simple fatigue that comes out of a difference of opinion. It's Goddamn tiring to have a difference of opinion. Someone comes in and says, "I hate to tell you, but this room we're sitting in is supposed to look like 1933 and it looks like 1945." It's tiring. You say, "Allright, move these couches out and get rid of that desk. Change the curtains." At a certain stage in life, at a certain point on the ladder of success, it is easier to say, "Look, I think it looks fine. Get the hell out of here. We are going to shoot it the way it is." That's why certain directors, and actors, eventually become old-fashioned. They cease to be willing to undertake the fatigue that's involved when there is a difference of opinion. And what else is making a movie, or any other attempt, except attention to detail? It is all detail, detail, detail. A hundred million, thousand, billion details. They are tiring, really tiring. When it's raining and your girl friend or your wife is saying, "Why aren't you doing such and such?" and the person you are working with has to go home

and return a call to his press agent, and lunch is being served, and the head of the union says, "Well, you have to stay out there for another ten minutes because they have to have coffee", and then the camera breaks down, and there is sound noise, a plane flying over, and this wasn't the location that you wanted, but you didn't get the approval from the other person, and the studio is charging a 25% overhead in this particular case so you know that your last picture didn't make a dime and they are going to have you; with all this, are you going to have the energy to devote to the detail of saying, "That license plate is the wrong year"? That's where the stamina, the real fight comes in. That is what's tiring.

A couple of years ago, it became fashionable—one of the bad by-products of a rather good and healthy influence—to look at Italian movies and attribute them wholly to their directors. To De Sica, to Fellini, Visconti, Antonioni, Monnicelli. Not to the actors, not the producer, not the leading lady. You have this man, that's his film, that's his work of art. He comes in with eighteen cans of film under his arm the way that Sinclair Lewis would come in with a novel. Well, that's bullshit. Those pictures were made by directors, writers, and sound men and cameramen, and actors, and so forth. But suddenly it's Otto Preminger's *Hurry Sundown*. The directors are the stars. Then it became stylish to say that a film must be the expression of a single man's vision. Twenty million dollar visions. It's not healthy. You don't hear much about Fellini's writers, do you? They're there . . .

HANSON: *As a producer, how would you have this power structure? You are saying that it is as much out of balance now as it was in the days when the star system was flourishing.*

BEATTY: Once you have a certain amount of story committed to film, the studio, the financing group, is in a position of weakness. There has to be some sort of responsibility evidenced on the part of film-makers to do pretty much what they agreed to in advance. Making a really good film is a matter of meticulous planning in many areas. The greater amount of time that you have and the more takes that you do, the more attention you can pay to those details. If you let your energy level fall, if you get drunk or stay up all night and come in the next morning and have no energy, you are letting down the people with the money because you will do two set-ups in the time when you could have done six. As a producer, my intention is to get the best possible picture we can at the agreed upon figure. That will entitle me then to go on and do other stories at the agreed upon figures. I would like to take as much fear out of it as I can for the studio. There is always going to be a certain amount of fear, but that fear should not involve being lackadaisical with regard to time and equipment, and so forth. I don't want to just make *a* picture. I want to make more pictures. I don't think I can get that right without pretty much doing what I agreed to do. You've been on the set, watching us shoot. You know that there's not a scene that we have done that we couldn't do better by taking another day. And you know the directors and producers and actors who would have taken another day. But we're on schedule; not because we are apathetic, but because we made an agreement.

HANSON : *There is going to be a point, maybe not with this picture, when the director is going to come to you and say, "What I want here is a helicopter shot", where they are leaving the scene or something. And you are going to say, "We can't do that. It's too expensive. It would slow us up." Whatever. You are going to assert your will over his, because you are the producer and it is your responsibility to get it done for the agreed upon price in the agreed upon time.*

BEATTY : You talk like I'm going to be a producer! Sometimes as a producer you have to make choices on behalf of the financing group. If you see an opportunity to do something that will cost extra money, and it looks like it would be a good investment, then you should take it. Ultimately we are dealing in very gray areas. But you talk about asserting over a director?

HANSON : *There will be what you feel is a questionable excess that the director wants, and you are going to have to say, "No."*

BEATTY : With that type of director, I would hope to be employed as an actor who is told "Show up at 7.00," and "Shut up, and say your lines!" That type of director would never accept me as a producer. With a person like Arthur Penn a conflict like that would never come up. If Arthur wanted something then I'm sure he would be right. He's an extremely responsible, sane man. I wouldn't put myself in the position of producing a picture with someone who I didn't feel had that kind of health about him.

HANSON : *You are saying, then, that if it did come up with Arthur, if he wanted something that perhaps you didn't see the value of, you would have the confidence in him to give the go-ahead.*

BEATTY: Oh, yes. Absolutely. No question. Because my function then as a producer would be to get it for him as efficiently and economically as possible. And carping about it might destroy the impulse that made him want it. Among sane people, who have the same end in sight, there shouldn't be a battle for control. That to me is all Lillian Ross, an old-fashioned myth permeated by outsiders to be printed in the *New Yorker*. How can we best get this script onto film? To me the rules are, express your thoughts intelligently, and have respect for the other person. Don't involve yourself with people unless you respect them, and if you respect them, listen to what they say. And don't involve yourself with people unless they respect you; which is equally important. Then give yourself enough sleep, enough time, and enough energy to have the time to express what you feel. That's what makes it fun. If you don't have the time to get through these details, if you don't have the energy . . .

HANSON: *Would you ever produce a film in which you did not appear?*

BEATTY: I would do it for somebody that I love. Or if I knew a piece of material that needed to be done, maybe. But generally speaking, it is a rather thankless job. The producer is somehow the villain. I feel sorry for producers. But I would do it if it came to be that people didn't seem that interested in seeing my face on the screen, if I couldn't write and I couldn't direct and I couldn't act and I couldn't dance or sing or do something, yes, I would do it. I think I would do it. Maybe I would do it. No, I wouldn't do it.

ARTHUR PENN AS DIRECTOR

CURTIS LEE HANSON: *In looking at your pictures, I notice what would appear to be a definite leaning towards subjects that are distinctly a part of Americana. Is that a preference of yours?*

ARTHUR PENN: Yes, it is. The best way to make movies is out of the things you know. I have had many opportunities to make pictures in Europe, but I have never really felt confident about being able to find the European equivalent for what I know, although I have spent a great deal of time there. You have a sense about the appropriateness of something in your own country that you just don't have in any other country. That is one part. Also, until recently, I have always equated the American temperament with the kinetic temperament. Americans act out what they feel. They apply it. The whole mythology of the country is based on that—the West; the Western; the great men of action—which seems to me to be the basic stuff of which movies are made, the best of them. The third part is that I am worried about what is happening in the country. And maybe worry is a very good source from which to make or from which to try to make, art. What frightens you and concerns you is also a very good source of materials. So, I seem to have ended up sticking to American subjects.

HANSON : *What aspects of America are worrying you particularly as related to your own work?*

PENN : Well, in the relatively brief time of my life—the period I can remember most acutely being since the second world war to the present—from having been what seemed to me a genuinely generous out-reaching country, I think that we have slipped into being a country in a defensive posture, a giant constantly with its fists up. When, indeed, just the reverse is what would be the hope of the world; that is, an outgoing, more generous charactered country. I don't mean that in terms of aid so much as I do in terms of viewpoint politically. And I think that we have had the internal correlation to that. Internally, the country has gotten more restrictive. The voice of opposition has been stilled for the past ten, twelve, fifteen years. I remember a very militant and vivid time during the depression when I was growing up, which doesn't seem to me to be present now. The same impulse is in the kids. But they are expressing it in other ways—personal, individual ways—rather than as something which has to do with the fate of their country and their world. They have far greater concern with their own sense of truth as it relates immediately to them.

HANSON : *As opposed to movements?* ·

PENN : To movements or to feeling that a part of the American character is to be outspoken about your political opinion. I don't necessarily suggest movements as such. Movements on the whole bore me, in the same way that unions bore me. I sort of believe in unions, and yet every time I run into one, I am bored by it. Collective activity bores me. What I miss in myself and miss in the environment of the country is the outspokenness of a great number of individuals who are not necessarily sympathetic with each other, who are not coagulated into a movement, but who are addressing themselves to their times. This may be unfair to the young kids of today, but I feel that they have a certain despair or disbelief in their ability to effect change in the whole world. Consequently, they have chosen the field of concern to be themselves. Which is not to say I am opposed to that; I just miss the other.

HANSON: *When I said your films were distinctly American, I didn't mean as opposed to a picture that you might do in Europe, but I meant even opposed to a picture made in the United States by someone else, which could have been done in Europe. In your movies, not only the scenes, but the people involved in the particular situations are just the United States and not anywhere else. Unmistakably the United States.*

PENN: Yes, I think that would be true of me no matter where I made a picture, because specificity is one of my on-going concerns. I approach as many scenes as I can with the need to find *the* specific ingredient of *the* specific behaviors, and inevitably they would be American. If I did a love story it would be the story of a couple of American kids, even if I did it in Africa, or in Europe. It would inevitably be made up of the substance that I know, which is the peculiar American courting habits, the peculiar American way. I probably could do *Wuthering Heights* and make it look like Sherwood Anderson wrote it. That's the way it would come out. I always wanted to do *Wuthering Heights* actually.

HANSON: *What was it in* Bonnie and Clyde *that first intrigued you? Any particular aspects?*

PENN: I suppose I have always been involved with the outlaw to a pretty large extent; I can't say without admiration for them. Although I find myself offended at saying it, because I have a large belief in the law. But I respect the fact that when the law is odious or unfair or unlivable, that somebody breaks it. When enough people have broken it, the law accommodates itself to that and alters. The history of laws in this country is one of constant change based upon the fact that individuals either spoke out or acted against the oppressive laws, and, when sufficient numbers did that, the laws eventually were altered. It is a part of the vitality of a democracy. Now I know it's absurd to be applying it to Bonnie and Clyde because I don't think of them as being in any sense the noble outlaw of the breed of Robin Hood or William Tell, who were speaking out against oppression. On the other hand, I do think they were a product of their times. I put psychology aside because I don't know what their psychology was, but let's just view them as historical figures in the social-political situation in which they found themselves. The country was destitute, in the grips of a depression which was not only economic, but was also a state of mind. It was a paralysed country. I can remember that, to a certain small extent from when I was very young, during the period, I remember the nature of the paralysis. I remember the universality of fear in the country. Bonnie and Clyde grew up in an essentially agricultural area where the banks were, because they had no other choice, foreclosing on homes and farms. Money had disappeared. In the film I don't mean to suggest that there was a villainy on the part of the banks. They were following their course in history. A time had come when the money that was available had fallen into the hands of a relatively small group of people. The rest of the country was suffering violently. They were still proceeding on the lines of an affluent democracy, acquisitive free enterprise, except the people who were the majority of the country were not free to have enterprise. The enterprise had disappeared. And I suppose that what intrigued me was the enterprise of Bonnie and Clyde, the bravura with which they decided to assault the system. And I have to say again and again, I don't mean to suggest that they had heroic character, because I don't believe that they did. But if they didn't, I wish that Bonnie and Clyde had had it, and I certainly mean that they should have it in this film. Which is *that* aspect of heroism which only history deposits on a character, a character who may have been purely villainous. In that sense, Robin Hood may have been nothing more than a bandit. William Tell may have been merely an insurrectionist. But, as we now view it, they served a very great end, by calling attention to grave injustice. And I think that is true of the time of Bonnie and Clyde. There were grave in-

185

justices being committed; not wilfully, perhaps. But there were people unable to alter the course on which they found themselves. I think it took Roosevelt to really alter the frame of mind of the country, and then consquently all the other things followed—the economic changes, the social changes, and consequently, the psychological changes. That part of *Bonnie and Clyde* interests me, as Billy the Kid interested me in *The Left-Handed Gun*. As Annie Sullivan interested me in *The Miracle Worker*; the person who comes up against 2,000 years of history, the fact that you cannot get through to a deaf-blind person, and who just says, "That is not necessarily the order of things", and does it. That is pretty inspiring stuff.

HANSON: *Your comments on the law-breaker as opposed to the law are interesting when applied to the characters in* The Chase. *There you have the one lawman as the sympathetic character of the picture.*

PENN: At the expense of sounding a sophist, in the peculiar inversion of that story, the defender of the law was the outlaw. The pure distillation of that story is that the sheriff does not act on all the available channels of action that are usually followed by the law in authority. That is, he didn't go out and muscle, he didn't go out and force, he didn't go out and organize posses and whoop up a great to-do. He believed in a certain tranquillity of the law. That the other members of the community didn't share his view was the sadness, and, if there is any tragedy in that picture, the tragedy. It is essentially the same story, only in that case it happens to be about a lawman rather than an outlaw.

HANSON: Bonnie and Clyde *is a picture particularly suited to you. You have a talent, and it would appear an inclination, for dealing with stories in terms of violence. Is this a conscious thing on your part?*

PENN: It wasn't. I wasn't aware of it until after I had done my first picture. I remember I went to see it with my sister-in-law and my brother. They both said, "My God, what a violent picture." Now it hadn't seemed at all violent to me in the making. However, when they said it, of course, I could see it. You don't have an awful lot of pictures where somebody gets blown apart with a shotgun, and six or seven other people are mowed down, and the hero is killed at the end without a gun in his hand, and so forth. So I began to be conscious of it and the more conscious of it I became, the more I just had to accept the fact: I like violence. I just like it. I think it makes good movies. It is as simple as that. I don't particularly, for instance, pursue it on the stage. I do rather contemplative, internal, serious plays in which violence hardly ever figures. So it is not that violence is essentially a part of my personality when I am working in the movies. I like violence in the movies. I think that movies are kinetic. I am a great admirer of Orson Welles, and he did that very well. Almost better than anybody I ever saw. When Kane wrecks that room near the end of *Citizen Kane* it is a massive upheaval. It is violence in the way that an earthquake is violent. I like to find myself doing that part for the movies. I just enjoy it.

HANSON: *Did you always intend to do movies?*

PENN: No, the reverse. I never thought I would be doing them.

HANSON: *You were always thinking in terms of the stage?*

PENN: Yes, stage, and at that time the way to get on the stage was to do television, so I began to learn about cameras and that sort of thing. But I never took the movies seriously until I was making my first picture. Then I discovered that I was having an absolutely marvelous time, to my great surprise and chagrin, because I had always sort of put the movies down. I didn't go to a lot of movies as a kid. It was different from the volume of experience of most people. Many of your generation, and of my generation, grew up running to the movies as the last haven, the retreat. A place where fantasies could be acted out, and so forth. But when I was very young I went to the movies and got frightened by a picture, and I didn't go back until I was fifteen. I didn't see *any* movies for ten years.

HANSON: *What was the picture?*

PENN: I cannot remember for the life of me. All I remember is going under my seat, and not coming out until it was over. Just scared out of my mind. Then, when I got to be fifteen, I would only go to relatively frivolous movies. It wasn't until I saw *Citizen Kane* that I thought that movies were anything at all. And *that* staggered me. From then on I began to have an interest in movies similar to my interest in the stage. In recent years, the balance is clearly switching to movies from the stage. But it has taken me longer. I seem to be maturing about movies later than most people.

HANSON: *Were there any other directors that had great impact on you during that time?*

PENN: Yes, but I didn't know them individually. It's peculiar. You see I had an almost phobic response to movies. I didn't know that there were separate studios, for instance, for years. I didn't know what Warner Brothers or Columbia meant. It sounds absolutely nuts, and it probably is, but I didn't know there was any difference. I just thought that all pictures were made in Hollywood and that they put these stamps on them for some reason or another. I wasn't conscious of a single director until Welles, and I was conscious of Welles only because he had come from radio and the theater.

HANSON: *You knew of him going in, then.*

PENN: Yes, I would be hard pressed to tell you of individual directors who impressed me. Although now I know the good ones, the ones who did the great films. Like Wellman; he absolutely knocked me out with *The Ox-Bow Incident*. Howard Hawks, with a number of pictures, but *Red River* just floored me. Hitchcock; I suppose if I really stopped and thought, I could go back and recall them, but I have to recall them in an inverted manner; I have to remember the movie and then who did it, rather than the other way around. Rather than being conscious of it at the time.

HANSON: *So that, actually, by the time you found yourself making your first picture, you had very little in the way of any movie background.*

PENN: None. Really none.

HANSON: *Necessity forced you to find your own technique.*

PENN: That was what it really amounted to, finding my own. I was not alert to what other people were doing in films when I started. It's only recently that I have come to be concerned and aware of what the other guys are doing. I did *Left-Handed Gun* during a period when I was doing a lot of television and I hadn't yet done a play. *Left-Handed Gun* was something of an unhappy experience for me in that, when the picture came out here, it was not at all successful. That bothered me and I thought that Warner Brothers didn't like it, and that maybe I didn't know how to make any kind of movies that they would like. So I left the picture business having made one picture, and went into the theater. I did five plays in a row in two years, and they were mercifully all hits, and I was just thinking that that was about the greatest experience

188

I had ever had in my life. Then I began to hear from Europe about *The Left-Handed Gun*. Somebody, quite by accident, sent somebody else a clipping out of a Belgian paper who in turn gave it to somebody else quite by accident, who in turn gave it to me. I read it, and I couldn't believe that they *admired* the picture. Not only admired it, but saw in it some of the things which I had intended. I have to preface this by saying that when the picture came out here, the *New York Times* absolutely loathed it and dismissed it as one of the real pieces of nonsense that Hollywood had ever made.

HANSON: *Was that a typical domestic review?*

PENN: No, not typical; the picture was hardly reviewed at all. But somebody at the *New York Times* just loathed it, and put it down in a very, almost ugly fashion. Then these things began to come from Europe, and when Truffaut began to write about it, and André Bazin began to talk about it, it absolutely staggered me. It rekindled my interest in film. So that when I went to make *The Miracle Worker,* I was beginning to be alert to the potency of directing films in a way that I had never been before.

HANSON: *You learned the camera in live television?*

PENN: Yes. I knew enough about the camera from television not to feel paralysed by it. Interestingly enough, I have grown less original with a camera rather than more, and I have to work against that.

HANSON: *That's very similar to something Welles said a while back. He said he could only have made* Citizen Kane *because it was his first movie and he didn't yet know what was impossible. He didn't know what couldn't be done.*

PENN: That's very true. Everyone wishes for that first innocence. It is marvelous to have. You feel like you can do anything. And go anywhere.

HANSON: *Faye remarked to me the other day that you had said you were learning more on this picture than you had on all your previous ones.*

PENN: Yes. That bears reference to what I just said. I am trying to educate myself *back* into using the camera more inventively than I have in the last couple of pictures. You don't know that you are aware of it, you are a victim of orthodoxy. I am forcing myself in this picture to try and open it up and get away from it. Now I am not succeeding wholly yet, but I am getting there.

189

HANSON: *Trying to unlearn.*

PENN: Trying to unlearn, and to open the doors of vision a little more broadly than they ordinarily are in a picture.

HANSON: *Going at it with that attitude, how do you work with your cinematographer?*

PENN: A cinematographer really does what you ask him to do, and he does it either very well or less well or poorly. Guffey is a good man and does it well.

HANSON: *It is your relationship to the story then?*

PENN: Yes. It is a question of the vision of the material and how to see it. It's *that* part of it that I have to deal with, that I have to train myself to deal with. And I could do it more; I should do it more; I will do it more. But I have become a little bit intimidated by the sheer excellence of films; the excellence of the Hollywood technique. It is on the one hand very supportive, but on the other hand it sort of narcotizes you, and you stop thinking. It becomes a superb machine for photographing a scene in a perfectly sound and reasonable way and it alleviates you of making a visual commitment which says that there is a *single* way to see this scene and *only* a single way. I did that in the beginning, and I have done it less and less, and I should go back to doing it. Hitchcock does it superbly. And it is to be respected. It is something I have to do more of and better. I am trying on this picture.

HANSON: *Is it something you can be specific about? What unorthodox aspects of the camera interest you in regard to a particular scene?*

PENN: A scene that takes place in the movies tends to become very much like a scene in a play, with the camera becoming the proscenium. You photograph it in a master shot, and then you photograph it in a medium shot, and then you photograph it in individual shots, and that scene is done, in quotes, "covered". Now, that's true. It *is* covered, and you do have the material to cut with, but I contend that if one could *really, really* dig in, that there is a *single* view of a given scene in a way that no multiplicity of angles will illuminate it. An example, for instance, is in *Citizen Kane* when Welles finally drops that camera and puts the lens at floor level. That is the only way in which that scene should be seen. That is a purely aesthetic decision he makes, culminating in that. You then don't do six or seven covering shots just in case that

190

doesn't work. You *know* that that worked. There was a scene in *The Miracle Worker,* a modified crane shot, in which the crane just leapt around following Patti Duke as she went from perception to perception right after she learned that there was such a thing as language. And everybody said, "That's going to be just sickening to watch on the screen; just nauseous; the camera moves so fast it will destroy the effect". It turned out that that was the way it *had* to be seen. If you have the time to prepare a movie, and you prepare it well; if you can summon it up, at least for the major scenes, there is a single particular *distilled* viewpoint that you should have. And all the coverage in the world will not improve that, if you get it right.

HANSON: *And that one viewpoint would exist without cutting.*

PENN: Probably without cutting. It would be the purest single way to see that scene. Cutting is another part of the world. It is a very exciting part, but it is also, in a certain sense, a crutch. Cutting edits out the unwanted, as much as it edits in the wanted. You should be able to get a sense from such a viewpoint that all is wanted to be seen, is seen, without the emphasis of cutting. Now maybe that is a purity that is unachievable, but I can remember occasions when I have seen that nearly achieved. In Welles. In Hitchcock. In Eisenstein.

HANSON: *In Ford, certainly.*

PENN: Ford! In Ford, many, many times. See there, I must have seen ten Ford pictures before I knew John Ford's name. I just didn't know his name.

HANSON: *How do you feel, carrying along the idea of a single viewpoint, about the actors? Do you feel it is advantageous for the performance to do it from one angle, one take, rather than going for coverage?*

PENN: Yes, I do. If you can find the right aspect, it is best to have it in one experience, in one flow of emotion. It is clear that, if you shoot the master shot in the morning, and the close-up in the evening of the same day, something qualitatively has changed in terms of the actor. How much better to be able to get it all! But there are a number of things which militate against that. One is that the director often does not, or cannot achieve that. Two, the excessively high technical standards of Hollywood make it difficult. For example, Hollywood lights perfectly, for *one* angle. To do a scene in one take would probably violate that single angle. I would be content with much sloppier film, less technically perfect film, than Hollywood seems to be prepared to be content with. Three, the equipment militates against it. Given the incredible advances in the qualities of the new films, to be operating movies out of that old black Mitchell camera, that antique of the 30s, is as absurd as almost anything I know. A good camera is needed that would be lightweight, vital, fast, mobile. Really at the service of the scene, rather than the scene at the service of the camera. This nonsense of the actors having to hit marks and so forth because the man who is operating the camera cannot see through the camera, and the man who is changing focus cannot see what is happening, but has to relate to where the actors stand on the floor, is absolutely absurd. Just absurd. If the studios got together with an absolutely minimal expenditure of money, they could perfect a camera that would do all those things and still get a very high quality film.

HANSON : *Why hasn't it been done?*

PENN : Until recently Hollywood never felt the need to do it. Until the television incursion, Hollywood was perfectly content to go on using the camera that they had. There was no competition. Nobody was knocking at the door. Since then, and since the expansion of European films and since the development of technique in Europe which grew out of poverty, rather than out of riches, there has been a certain concern in Hollywood. They will do it, sooner or later. All I know is that right now, on this picture, we are using a camera that was made in 1932 or 1933. That seems to me bizarre.

HANSON : *How fitting for* Bonnie and Clyde.

PENN : Yes! It is a period camera. I can't think of another industry in which the essential tool was designed in 1932 and has remained exactly that way. Not the telephone, not the aviation industry, not anything.

HANSON : *Having had so much stage experience, it must be frustrating not to be able to extensively rehearse the actors when working in film.*

PENN : Very. Rehearsing gets to be less and less possible. All the union rules are a great hindrance. When an actor does not start in a picture for five or six weeks, if you brought him in for rehearsal before you started shooting, you would have to be paying him all that time. I think the Screen Actors Guild does itself an enormous disservice. Rehearsal is extremely valuable. You just don't discover everything there is to be discovered about a scene in the few minutes before you shoot it. It's not possible. Consequently, it means that you have to come on the set with a certain number of devised tricks which closes you off from what you and the actors might be able to invent given enough time to grow familiar with the material. I don't know very many actors who can exist without rehearsal, but almost all of them try to do it, and seem content.

HANSON : *To overcome this inability to rehearse, how do you work with your actors? Is there a method that you can verbalize?*

PENN : Gee, it's hard. I guess there are two things I try to work for. One is to address an actor to what the scene requirements are, to fulfil whatever the story requires at that point, with sufficient relaxation and sufficient ease to permit accidents to occur. The other is to keep them from feeling that an accident is a mistake. The accidents are the human behavior.

HANSON : *You would then try and get actors with whom the accidents would happen.*

PENN : Yes. Or at least they would be such that they would be usable and wouldn't throw the actor, or wouldn't cause the others to stop. Most actors come on a movie set and have the lines and the marks and the actions clearly in mind and they do them, and if there is any variation from that, they stop, or they come apart. I hope that slowly we are learning about each other enough to admit the unexpected. The unexpected is what makes for good acting. You should be free enough to say, "Whatever you do, I will be able to respond to as the character, because nothing I do will be un-characteristic". By that I mean that the actor playing the role *is* the character. There is nobody else. There is no Bonnie. There is no Clyde. Except Faye and Warren. Whatever they do is Bonnie and Clyde. It just is. Now whether it is the Bonnie and Clyde of our story or not is another question, and at that level I would try to help them make a selection. But I could wish that they would be free enough to feel that whatever they would do or think would belong. And that's basically the way I try to work with all my actors.

HANSON : *Which again would indicate one take, if possible.*

PENN : Exactly. In the best of all worlds.

HANSON : *Warren, I know, has very fixed ideas about the group*

193

effort involved in making pictures—the co-operation between all the different elements, the writers, cameramen, director, actors, producer. I'm curious as to whether you think that is reconcilable with what you were saying about movies having a single strong viewpoint.

PENN: I would say that we are really talking about two different types of film there. Warren's concept of the group as such is a way of making good, successful pictures. I would put the emphasis on successful. The other way may not necessarily result in *successful* (if successful is equated with money), films. I think they would be better films. I subscribe in that sense to the *auteur* theory, in that film is really one man's form. It just is. There seems to me to be no doubt about that. Entertainment films are group efforts and they had better be group efforts. The wonderful thing about the people in the entertainment world is how superb they are at what their speciality is. They work together and make a good show. But a movie may be a very bad show and be a wonderful movie. Like *400 Blows* I would not think of as a good show, but it is a wonderful movie. Godard's films are not good shows, in that they are not consistently high level in entertainment. He varies them and twists them and turns them. But they are damn good movies . . . A movie is really an act of passion. It's the hardest work I know. You should be doing it not for money, but for passion. Fortunately, I am able to say that I have a lot of passion about this picture, and I hope that it gets on the screen. I don't know of harder work in the world, I swear I don't. Physically harder, emotionally harder, more single minded.

Extracts from two interviews which first appeared in Cinema *(U.S.), Vol. 3, No. 5. Reproduced by permission.*

Pauline Kael

CRIME AND POETRY

How do you make a good movie in this country without being jumped on? *Bonnie and Clyde* is the most excitingly American movie since *The Manchurian Candidate*. The audience is alive to it. Our experience as we watch it has some connection with the way we react to movies in childhood : with how we came to love them and we feel they were ours — not an art that we learned over the years to appreciate, but simply and immediately ours. When an American movie is contemporary in feeling, like this one, it makes a different kind of contact with an American audience from the kind that is made by European films, however contemporary. Yet any movie that is contemporary in feeling is likely to go further than other movies — go too far for some tastes — and *Bonnie and Clyde* divides audiences, as *The Manchurian Candidate* did, and it is being jumped on almost as hard. Though we may dismiss the attacks with "What good movie doesn't give some offense?" the fact that it is generally *only* good movies that provoke attacks by many people suggests that the innocuousness of our movies is accepted with such complacence that when an American movie reaches people, when it makes them react, some of them think there must be something the matter with it — perhaps a law should be passed against it. *Bonnie and Clyde* brings into the almost frighteningly public world of movies things that people have been feeling and saying and writing about, and once something is said or done on the screens of the world, once it has entered mass art, it can never again belong to a minority, never again be the private possession of an educated, or "knowing," group. But even for that group there is an excitement in hearing its own private thoughts expressed out loud and in seeing something of its own sensibility become part of our common culture.

Our best movies have always made entertainment out of the anti-heroism of American life; they bring to the surface what, in its newest forms and fashions, is always just below the surface. The romanticism in American movies lies in the cynical tough guy's independence; the sentimentality lies, traditionally, in the falsified mentality when the anti-hero turns hero. In 1967, this kind of

195

sentimentality wouldn't work with the audience, and *Bonnie and Clyde* substitutes sexual fulfilment for a change of heart. (This doesn't quite work, either; audiences sophisticated enough to enjoy a movie like this one are too sophisticated for the dramatic uplift of the triumph over impotence.)

Structurally, *Bonnie and Clyde* is a story of love on the run, like the old Clark Gable-Claudette Colbert *It Happened One Night* but turned inside out; the walls of Jericho are psychological this time, but they fall anyway. If the story of Bonnie Parker and Clyde Barrow seemed almost from the start, and even to them while they were living it, to be the material of legend, it's because robbers who are loyal to each other — like the James brothers — are a grade up from garden-variety robbers, and if they're male and female partners in crime and young and attractive they're a rare breed. The Barrow gang had both family loyalty and sex appeal working for their legend. David Newman and Robert Benton, who wrote the script for *Bonnie and Clyde,* were able to use the knowledge that, like many of our other famous outlaws and gangsters, the real Bonnie and Clyde seemed to others to be acting out forbidden roles and to relish their roles. In contrast with secret criminals — the furtive embezzlers and other crooks who lead seemingly honest lives — the known outlaws capture the public imagination, because they take chances, and because, often, they enjoy dramatizing their lives. They know that newspaper readers want all the details they can get about the criminals who do the terrible things they themselves don't dare to do, and also want the satisfaction of reading about the punishment after feasting on the crimes. Outlaws play to this public; they show off their big guns and fancy clothes and their defiance of the law. Bonnie and Clyde established the images for their own legend in the photographs they posed for: the gunman and the gun moll. The naïve, touching doggerel ballad that Bonnie Parker wrote and had published in newspapers is about the roles they play for other people contrasted with the coming end for them. It concludes:

> Someday they'll go down together;
> They'll bury them side by side;
> To few it'll be grief —
> To the law a relief —
> But it's death for Bonnie and Clyde.

196

That they did capture the public imagination is evidenced by the many movies based on their lives. In the late forties, there were *They Live By Night,* with Farley Granger and Cathy O'Donnell, and *Gun Crazy,* with John Dall and Peggy Cummins. (Alfred Hitchcock, in the same period, cast these two Clyde Barrows, Dall and Granger, as Loeb and Leopold, in *Rope.*) And there was a cheap — in every sense — 1958 exploitation film, *The Bonnie Parker Story,* starring Dorothy Provine. But the most important earlier version was Fritz Lang's *You Only Live Once,* starring Sylvia Sidney as "Joan" and Henry Fonda as "Eddie", which was made in 1937; this version, which was one of the best American films of the thirties, as *Bonnie and Clyde* is of the sixties, expressed certain feelings of its time, as this film expresses certain feelings of ours. (*They Live By Night,* produced by John Houseman under the aegis of Dore Schary, and directed by Nicholas Ray, was a very serious and socially significant tragic melodrama, but its attitudes were already dated thirties attitudes: the lovers were very young and pure and frightened and underprivileged; the hardened criminals were sordid; the settings were committedly grim. It made no impact on the postwar audience, though it was a great success in England, where our mouldy socially significant movies could pass for courageous.)

Just how contemporary in feeling *Bonnie and Clyde* is may be indicated by contrasting it with *You Only Live Once,* which, though almost totally false to the historical facts, was told straight. It is a peculiarity of our times — perhaps it's one of the few specifically modern characteristics — that we don't take our stories straight anymore. This isn't necessarily bad. *Bonnie and Clyde* is the first film demonstration that the put-on can be used for the purposes of art. *The Manchurian Candidate* almost succeeded in that, but what was implicitly wild and far out in the material was nevertheless presented on screen as a straight killer. *Bonnie and Clyde* keeps the audience in a kind of eager, nervous imbalance — holds our attention by throwing our disbelief back in our faces. To be put on is to be put on the spot, put on the stage, made the stooge in a comedy act. People in the audience at *Bonnie and Clyde* are laughing, demonstrating that they're not stooges — that they appreciate the joke — when they catch the first bullet right in the face. The movie keeps them off balance to the end. During

197

the first part of the picture, a woman in my row was gleefully assuring her companions, "It's a comedy. It's a comedy." After a while, she didn't say anything. Instead of the movie spoof, which tells the audience that it doesn't need to feel or care, that it's all just in fun, that "we were only kidding," *Bonnie and Clyde* disrupts us with "And you thought we were only kidding."

This is the way the story was told in 1937. Eddie (Clyde) is a three-time loser who wants to work for a living, but nobody will give him a chance. Once you get on the wrong side of the law, "they" won't let you get back. Eddie knows it's hopeless —once a loser, always a loser. But his girl, Joan (Bonnie) — the only person who believes in him — thinks that an innocent man has nothing to fear. She marries him, and learns better. Arrested again and sentenced to death for a crime he didn't commit, Eddie asks her to smuggle a gun to him in prison, and she protests, "If I get you a gun, you'll kill somebody." He stares at her sullenly and asks, "What do you think they're going to do to me?" He becomes a murderer while escaping from prison; "society" has made him what it thought he was all along. *You Only Live Once* was an indictment of "society", of the forces of order that will not give Eddie the outcast a chance. "We have a right to live," Joan says as they set out across the country. During the time they are on the run, they become notorious outlaws; they are blamed for a series of crimes they didn't commit. (They do commit holdups, but only to get gas or groceries or medicine.) While the press pictures them as desperadoes robbing and killing and living high on the proceeds of crime, she is having a baby in a shack in a hobo jungle, and Eddie brings her a bouquet of wild flowers. Caught in a police trap, they die in each other's arms; they have been denied the right to live.

Because *You Only Live Once* was so well done, and because the audience in the thirties shared this view of the indifference and cruelty of "society", there were no protests against the sympathetic way the outlaws were pictured — and, indeed there was no reason for any. In 1958, in *I Want To Live!* (a very popular, though not very good, movie), Barbara Graham, a drug-addict prostitute who had been executed for her share in the bludgeoning to death of an elderly woman, was presented as gallant, wronged, morally superior to everybody else in the movie, in order to strengthen

198

the argument against capital punishment, and the director, Robert Wise, and his associates weren't accused of glorifying criminals, because the "criminals", as in *You Only Live Once*, weren't criminals but innocent victims. Why the protests, why are so many people upset (and not just the people who enjoy indignation), about *Bonnie and Clyde,* in which the criminals *are* criminals — Clyde an ignorant, sly near-psychopath who thinks his crimes are accomplishments, and Bonnie a bored, restless waitress-slut who robs for excitement? And why so many accusations of historical inaccuracy, particularly against a work that is far more accurate historically than most and in which historical accuracy hardly matters anyway? There is always an issue of historical accuracy involved in any dramatic or literary work set in the past; indeed, it's fun to read about Richard III vs Shakespeare's Richard III. The issue is always with us, and will always be with us as long as artists find stimulus in historical figures and want to present their versions of them. But why didn't movie critics attack, for example, *A Man For All Seasons* — which involves material of much more historical importance — for being historically inaccurate? Why attack *Bonnie and Clyde* more than the other movies based on the same pair, or more than the movie treatments of Jesse James or Billy the Kid or Dillinger or Capone or any of our other fictionalized outlaws? I would suggest that when a movie so clearly conceived as a new version of a legend is attacked as historically inaccurate, it's because it shakes people a little. I know this is based on some pretty sneaky psychological suppositions, but I don't see how else to account for the use only against a *good* movie of arguments that could be used against almost all movies. When I asked a nineteen-year-old boy who was raging against the movie as "a cliché-ridden fraud" if he got so worked up about other movies, he informed me that that was an argument *ad hominem*. And it is indeed. To ask why people react so angrily to the best movies and have so little negative reaction to poor ones is to imply that they are so unused to the experience of art in movies that they fight it.

Audiences at *Bonnie and Clyde* are not given a simple, secure basis for identification; they are made to feel but are not told how to feel. *Bonnie and Clyde* is not a serious melodrama involving us in the plight of the innocent but a movie that assumes — as

199

William Wellman did in 1931 when he made *Public Enemy,* with James Cagney as a smart, cocky, mean little crook — that we don't need to pretend we're interested only in the falsely accused, as if real criminals had no connection with us. There wouldn't be the popular excitement there is about outlaws if we didn't all suspect that — in some cases, at least — gangsters must take pleasure in the profits and glory of a life of crime. Outlaws wouldn't become legendary figures if we didn't suspect that there's more to crime than the social workers' case studies may show. And though what we've always been told will happen to them — that they'll come to a bad end — does seem to happen, some part of us wants to believe in the tiny possibility that they can get away with it. Is that really so terrible? Yet when it comes to movies people get nervous about acknowledging that there must be some fun in crime (though the gleam in Cagney's eye told its own story). *Bonnie and Clyde* shows the fun but uses it, too, making comedy out of the banality and conventionality of that fun. What looks ludicrous in this movie isn't *merely* ludicrous, and after we have laughed at ignorance and helplessness and emptiness and stupidity and idiotic devilry, the laughs keep sticking in our throats, because what's funny isn't only funny.

In 1937, the movie-makers knew that the audience wanted to believe in the innocence of Joan and Eddie, because these two were lovers, and innocent lovers hunted down like animals made a tragic love story. In 1967, the movie-makers know that the audience wants to believe — maybe even prefers to believe — that Bonnie and Clyde were guilty of crimes, all right, but that they were innocent in general; that is, naïve and ignorant *compared with us.* The distancing of the sixties version shows the gangsters in an already legendary period, and part of what makes a legend for Americans is viewing anything that happened in the past as much simpler than what we are involved in now. We tend to find the past funny and the recent past campy-funny. The getaway cars of the early thirties are made to seem hilarious. (Imagine anyone getting away from a bank holdup in a tin Lizzie like that!) In *You Only Live Once,* the outlaws existed in the same present as the audience, and there was (and still is, I'm sure) nothing funny about them; in *Bonnie and Clyde* that audience is in the movie, transformed into the poor people, the Depression people, of legend

— with faces and poses out of Dorothea Lange and Walker Evans and *Let Us Now Praise Famous Men*. In 1937, the audience felt sympathy for the fugitives because they weren't allowed to lead normal lives; in 1967, the "normality" of the Barrow gang and their individual aspirations toward respectability are the craziest things about them — not just because they're killers but because thirties "normality" is in itself funny to us. The writers and the director of *Bonnie and Clyde* play upon our attitudes toward the American past by making the hats and guns and holdups look as dated as two-reel comedy; emphasizing the absurdity with banjo music, they make the period seem even farther away than it is. The Depression reminiscences are not used for purposes of social consciousness; hard times are not the reason for the Barrows' crimes, just the excuse. "We" didn't make Clyde a killer; the movie deliberately avoids easy sympathy by picking up Clyde when he is already a cheap crook. But Clyde is not the urban sharpster of *Public Enemy;* he is the hick as bank robber — a countrified gangster, a hillbilly killer who doesn't mean any harm. People so simple that they are alienated from the results of their actions — like the primitives who don't connect babies with copulation — provide a kind of archetypal comedy for us. It may seem like a minor point that Bonnie and Clyde are presented as not mean and sadistic, as having killed only when cornered; but in terms of legend, and particularly movie legend, it's a major one. The "classic" gangster films showed gang members betraying each other and viciously murdering the renegade who left to join another gang; the gang leader hero no sooner got to the top than he was betrayed by someone he had trusted or someone he had double-crossed. In contrast, the Barrow gang represents family-style crime. And Newman and Benton have been acute in emphasizing this — not making them victims of society (they are never that, despite Penn's cloudy efforts along these lines) but making them absurdly "just-folks" ordinary. When Bonnie tells Clyde to pull off the road — "I want to talk to you" — they are in a getaway car, leaving the scene of the robbery, with the police right behind them, but they are absorbed in family bickering : the traditional all-American use of the family automobile. In a sense, it is the absence of sadism — it is the violence without sadism — that throws the audience off balance at *Bonnie and Clyde*. The brutality that comes out of this

201

innocence is far more shocking than the calculated brutalities of mean killers.

Playfully posing with their guns, the real Bonnie and Clyde mocked the "Bloody Barrows" of the Hearst press. One photograph shows slim, pretty Bonnie, smiling and impeccably dressed, pointing a huge gun at Clyde's chest as he, a dimpled dude with a cigar, smiles back. The famous picture of Bonnie in the same clothes but looking ugly squinting into the sun, with a foot on the car, a gun on her hip, and a cigar in her mouth, is obviously a joke — her caricature of herself as a gun moll. Probably, since they never meant to kill, they thought the "Bloody Barrows" were a joke — a creation of the lying newspapers.

There's something new and good working for the Bonnie-and-Clyde legend now: our nostalgia for the thirties — the unpredictable, contrary affection of the prosperous for poverty, or at least for the artifacts, the tokens, of poverty, for Pop culture seen in the dreariest rural settings, where it truly seems to belong. Did people in the cities listen to the Eddie Cantor show? No doubt they did, but the sound of his voice, like the sound of Ed Sullivan now, evokes a primordial, pre-urban existence — the childhood of the race. Our comic-melancholic affection for thirties Pop has become sixties Pop, and those who made *Bonnie and Clyde* are smart enough to use it that way. Being knowing is not an artist's highest gift, but it can make a hell of a lot of difference in a movie. In the American experience, the miseries of the Depression are funny in the way that the Army is funny to draftees — a shared catastrophe, a leveling, forming part of our common background. Those too young to remember the Depression have heard about it from their parents. (When I was at college, we used to top each other's stories about how our families had survived: the fathers who had committed suicide so that their wives and children could live off the insurance; the mothers trying to make a game out of the meals of potatoes cooked on an open fire.) Though the American derision of the past has many offensive aspects, it has some good ones, too, because it's a way of making fun not only of our forebears but of ourselves and our pretensions. The toughness about what we've come out of and what we've been through — the honesty to see ourselves as the Yahoo children of yokels — is a good part of American poetry in a stickup gang seen chasing across the

202

bedraggled backdrop of the Depression (as true in its way as Nabokov's vision of Humbert Humbert and Lolita in the cross-country world of motels) — as if crime were the only activity in a country stupefied by poverty. But Arthur Penn doesn't quite have the toughness of mind to know it; it's not what he means by poetry. His squatters' jungle scene is too "eloquent," like a poster making an appeal, and the Parker family reunion sequence is poetic in the gauzy mode. He makes the sequence a fancy lyric interlude, like a number in a musical (*Funny Face,* to be exact); it's too "imaginative" — a literal dust bowl, as thoroughly becalmed as Sleeping Beauty's garden. The movie becomes dreamy-soft where it should be hard (and hard-edged).

If there is such a thing as an American tragedy, it must be funny. O'Neill undoubtedly felt this when he had James Tyrone get up to turn off the lights in *Long Day's Journey Into Night.* We are bumpkins, haunted by the bottle of ketchup on the dining table at San Simeon. We garble our foreign words and phrases and hope that at least we've used them right. Our heroes pick up the wrong fork, and the basic figure of fun in the American theater and American movies is the man who puts on airs. Children of peddlers and hod carriers don't feel at home in tragedy; we are used to failure. But, because of the quality of American life at the present time, perhaps there can be no real comedy — nothing more than stupidity and "spoof" — without true horror in it. Bonnie and Clyde and their partners in crime are comically bad bank robbers, and the backdrop of poverty makes their holdups seems pathetically tacky, yet they rob banks and kill people; Clyde and his good-natured brother are so shallow they never think much about anything, yet they suffer and die.

If this way of holding more than one attitude toward life is already familiar to us — if we recognize the make-believe robbers whose toy guns produce red blood, and the Keystone cops who shoot them dead, from Truffaut's *Shoot The Piano Player* and Godard's gangster pictures, *Breathless* and *Band of Outsiders* — it's because the young French directors discovered the poetry of crime in American life (from our movies) and showed the Americans how to put it on the screens in a new, "existential" way. Melodramas and gangster movies and comedies were always more our speed than "prestigious," "distinguished" pictures; the French directors who grew up on American pictures found poetry in our fast action, laconic speech, plain gestures. And because they understood that you don't express your love of life by denying the comedy or the horror of it, they brought out the poetry in our tawdry subjects. Now Arthur Penn, working with a script heavily influenced — one might almost say inspired — by Truffaut's *Shoot The Piano Player,* unfortunately imitates Truffaut's artistry instead of going back to its tough American sources. The French may tenderize their American material, but we shouldn't. That turns into another way of making "prestigious," "distinguished" pictures.

Probably part of the discomfort that people feel about *Bonnie and Clyde* grows out of its compromises and its failures. I wish the script hadn't provided the upbeat of the hero's sexual success as a kind of sop to the audience. I think what makes us not believe in it is that it isn't consistent with the intelligence of the rest of the writing — that it isn't on the same level, because it's too manipulatively clever, too much of a gimmick. (The scene that shows the gnomish gang member called C. W. sleeping in the same room as Bonnie and Clyde suggests other possibilities, perhaps discarded, as does C. W.'s reference to Bonnie's liking his tattoo.) Compromises are not new to the Bonnie-and-Clyde story; *You Only Live Once* had a tacked-on-coda featuring a Heavenly choir and William Gargan as a dead priest, patronizing Eddie even in the afterlife, welcoming him to Heaven with "You're free, Eddie!" The kind of people who make a movie like *You Only Live Once* are not the kind who write endings like that, and, by the same sort of internal evidence, I'd guess that Newman and Benton, whose Bonnie seems to owe so much to Catherine in *Jules and Jim,* had more interesting ideas originally about Bonnie's and Clyde's (and maybe C. W.'s) sex lives.

But people also feel uncomfortable about the violence, and here I think they're wrong. That is to say, they *should* feel uncomfortable, but this isn't an argument *against* the movie. Only a few years ago, a good director would have suggested the violence obliquely, with reaction shots (like the famous one in *The Golden Coach,* when we saw a whole bullfight reflected in Anna Magnani's face), and death might have been symbolized by a light going out, or stylized, with blood and wounds kept to a minimum. In many ways, this method is more effective; we feel the violence more because so much is left to our imaginations. But the whole point of *Bonnie and Clyde* is to rub our noses in it, to make us pay our dues for laughing. The dirty reality of death — not suggestions but blood and holes — is necessary. Though I generally respect a director's skill and intelligence in inverse ratio to the violence he shows on the screen, and though I questioned even the Annie Sullivan-Helen Keller fight scenes in Arthur Penn's *The Miracle Worker*, I think that this time Penn is right. (I think he was also right when he showed violence in his first film, *The Left-Handed Gun*, in 1958.) Suddenly, in the last few years, our view of the world has gone beyond "good taste." Tasteful suggestions of violence would at this point be a more grotesque form of comedy than *Bonnie and Clyde* attempts. *Bonnie and Clyde* needs violence; violence is its meaning. When, during a comically botched-up getaway, a man is shot in the face, the image is obviously based on one of the most famous sequences in Eisenstein's *Potemkin*, and the startled face is used the same way it was in *Potemkin* — to convey in an instant how someone who just happens to be in the wrong place at the wrong time, the irrelevant "innocent" bystander, can get it full in the face. And at that instant the meaning of Clyde Barrow's character changes; he's still a clown, but we've become the butt of the joke.

It is a kind of violence that says something to us; it is something that movies must be free to use. And it is just because artists must be free to use violence — a legal right that is beginning to come under attack — that we must also defend the legal rights of those film-makers who use violence to sell tickets, for it is not the province of the law to decide that one man is an artist and another man a no-talent. The no-talent has as much right to produce works as the artist has, and not only because he has a suprising way of shifting from one category to the other but also because men have an inalienable right to be untalented, and the law should not discriminate against lousy "artists". I am not saying that the violence in *Bonnie and Clyde* is legally acceptable because the film is a work of art; I think that *Bonnie and Clyde,* though flawed, is a work of art, but I think that the violence in *The Dirty Dozen,* which isn't a work of art, and whose violence offends me *personally,* should also be legally defensible, however morally questionable. Too many people — including some movie reviewers — want the law to take over the job of movie criticism; perhaps what they really want is for their own criticisms to have the force of law. Such people see *Bonnie and Clyde* as a danger to public morality; they think an audience goes to a play or a movie and takes the actions in it as examples for imitation. They look at the world and blame the movies. But if women who are angry with their husbands take it out on their kids, I don't think we can blame *Medea* for it; if, as has been said, we are a nation of mother-lovers, I don't think we can place the blame on *Oedipus Rex*. Part of the power of art lies in showing us what we are *not* capable of. We see that killers are not a different breed but are *us* without the insight or understanding or self-control that works of art strengthen. The tragedy of *Macbeth* is in the fall from nobility to horror; the comic tragedy of *Bonnie and Clyde* is that although you can't fall from the bottom you can reach the same horror. The movies may set styles in dress or love-making, they may advertise cars or beverages, but art is not examples for imitation — that is not what a work of art does for us — though that is what guardians of morality think art is and what they want it to be and why they think a good movie is one that sets "healthy," "cheerful" examples of behaviour, like a giant all-purpose commercial for the American way of life. But people don't buy what they see in a movie quite so simply; Louis B. Mayer did not turn us into a nation of Andy Hardy's, and if, in a film, we see a frightened man wantonly take the life of another, it does not encourage us to do the same, any more than seeing an ivory hunter shoot an elephant makes us want to shoot one. It may, on the contrary, so sensitize us that we get a pang in the gut if we accidentally step on a moth.

Will we, as some people have suggested, be lured into imitating the violent crimes of Clyde and Bonnie because Warren Beatty and Faye Dunaway are "glamorous"? Do they, as some people have charged, confer glamour on violence? It's difficult to see how, since the characters they play are horrified by it and ultimately destroyed by it. Nobody in the movie gets pleasure from violence. Is the charge based on the notion that simply by their presence in the movie Warren Beatty and Faye Dunaway make crime attractive? If movie stars can't play criminals without our all wanting to be criminals, then maybe the only safe roles for them to play are movie stars — which, in this assumption, everybody wants to be anyway. After all, if they played factory workers, the economy might be dislocated by everybody's trying to become a factory worker. (Would having criminals played by dwarfs or fatties discourage them? It seems rather doubtful.) The accusation that the beauty of movie stars makes the anti-social acts of their characters dangerously attractive is the kind of contrived argument we get from people who are bothered by something and are clutching at straws. Actors and actresses are *usually* more beautiful than ordinary people. And why not? Garbo's beauty notwithstanding, her Anna Christie did not turn us into whores, her Mata Hari did not turn us into spies, her Anna Karenina did not make us suicides. We did not want her to be ordinary looking. Why should we be deprived of the pleasure of beauty? Garbo could be all women in love because, being more beautiful than life, she could more beautifully express emotions. It is a supreme asset for actors and actresses to be beautiful; it gives them greater range and greater possibilities for expensiveness. The handsomer they are, the more roles they can play; Olivier can be anything, but who would want to see Ralph Richardson, great as he is, play Antony? Actors and actresses who are beautiful start with an enormous advantage, because we love to look at them. The joke in the glamour charge is that Faye Dunaway has the magazine-illustration look of countless uninterestingly pretty girls, and Warren Beatty has the kind of high-school good looks that are generally lost fast. It's the roles that make *them* seem glamorous. Good roles do that for actors.

There is a story told against Beatty in a recent *Esquire* — how during the shooting of *Lilith* he "delayed a scene for three days demanding the line 'I've read *Crime and Punishment* and *The Brothers Karamazov*' be changed to 'I've read *Crime and Punishment* and half of *The Brothers Karamazov*.'" Considerations of professional conduct aside, what is odd is why his adversaries waited three days to give in, because, of course, he was right. That's what the character he played *should* say; the other way, the line has no point at all. But this kind of intuition isn't enough to make an actor, and in a number of roles Beatty, probably because he doesn't have the technique to make the most of his lines in the least possible time, has depended too much on intuitive non-acting — holding the screen far too long as he acted out self-

207

preoccupied characters in a lifelike, boringly self-conscious way. He has a gift for slyness, though, as he showed in *The Roman Spring of Mrs. Stone*, and in most of his films he could hold the screen — maybe because there seemed to be something going on in his mind, some kind of calculation. There was something smart about him — something shrewdly private in those squeezed-up little non-actor's eyes — that didn't fit the clean-cut juvenile roles. Beatty was the producer of *Bonnie and Clyde*, responsible for keeping the company on schedule, and he has been quoted as saying, "There's not a scene that we have done that we couldn't do better by taking another day." This is the hell of the expensive way of making movies, but it probably helps to explain why Beatty is more intense than he has been before and why he has picked up his pace. His business sense may have improved his timing. The role of Clyde Barrow seems to have released something in him. As Clyde, Beatty is good with his eyes and mouth and his hat, but his body is still inexpressive; he doesn't have a trained actor's use of his body, and, watching him move, one is never for a minute convinced he's impotent. It is, however, a tribute to his performance that one singles this failure out. His slow timing works perfectly in the sequence in which he offers the dispossessed farmer his gun; there may not be another actor who would have dared to prolong the scene that way, and the prolongation until the final "We rob banks" gives the sequence the comic force. I have suggested elsewhere that one of the reasons that rules are impossible in the arts is that in movies (and in the other arts, too) the new "genius" — the genuine as well as the fraudulent or the dubious — is often the man who has enough audacity, or is simpleminded enough, to do what others had the good taste not to do. Actors before Brando did not mumble and scratch and show their sweat; dramatists before Tennessee Williams did not make explicit a particular substratum of American erotic fantasy; movie directors before Orson Welles did not dramatize the technique of film-making; directors before Richard Lester did not lay out the whole movie as cleverly as the opening credits; actresses before Marilyn Monroe did not make an asset of their ineptitude by turning faltering misreadings into an appealing style. Each, in a large way, did something that people had always enjoyed and were often embarrassed or ashamed about enjoying. Their "bad taste" shaped a new accepted taste. Beatty's non-actor's "bad" timing

208

may be this kind of "genius;" we seem to be watching him *think out* his next move.

It's difficult to know how Bonnie should have been played, because the character isn't worked out. Here the script seems weak. She is made too warmly sympathetic — and sympathetic in a style that antedates the style of the movie. Being frustrated and moody, she's not funny enough — neither ordinary, which, in the circumstances, would be comic, not perverse, which might be rather funny, too. Her attitude toward her mother is too loving. There could be something about her wanting to run home to her mama, but, as it has been done, her heading home, running off through the fields, is unconvincing — incompletely motivated. And because the element of the ridiculous that makes the others so individual has been left out of her characer she doesn't seem to belong to the period as the others do. Faye Dunaway has a sixties look anyway — not just because her eyes are made up in a sixties way and her hair is wrong but because her personal style and her acting are sixties. (This may help to make her popular; she can seem prettier to those who don't recognize prettiness except in the latest styles.) Furthermore, in some difficult-to-define way, Faye Dunaway as Bonnie doesn't keep her distance — that is to say, an *actor's* distance — either from the role or from the audience. She doesn't hold a characterization; she's in and out of emotions all the time, and though she often hits effective ones, the emotions seem *hers,* not the character's. She has some talent, but she comes on too strong; she makes one conscious that she's a willing worker, but she doesn't seem to know what she's doing — rather like Bonnie in her attempts to overcome Clyde's sexual difficulties.

Although many daily movie reviewers judge a movie in isolation, as if the people who made it had no previous history, more serious critics now commonly attempt to judge a movie as an expressive vehicle of the director, and a working out of his personal themes. Auden has written, "Our judgement of an established author is never simply an aesthetic judgement. In addition to any literary merit it may have, a new book by him has a historic interest for us as the act of a person in whom we have long been interested. He is not a poet . . . he is also a character in our biography." For a while, people went to the newest Bergman and the newest Fellini that way; these movies were greeted like the latest novels of a favourite author. But Arthur Penn is not a writer-director like Bergman or Fellini, both of whom began as writers, and who (even though Fellini employs several collaborators) compose their spiritual autobiographies step by step on film. Penn is far more dependent on the talents of others, and his primary material — what he starts with — does not come out of his own experience. If the popular audience is generally uninterested in the director (unless he is heavily publicized, like De Mille or Hitchcock), the audience that is interested in the art of movies has begun, with many of the critics, to think of movies as a director's medium to the point where they tend to ignore the contribution of the writers — and the directors may be almost obscenely content to omit mention of the writers. The history of the movies is being rewritten to disregard facts in favor of celebrating the director as the sole "creative" force. One can read Josef von Sternberg's autobiography and the text of the latest books on his movies without even finding the name of Jules Furthman, the writer who worked on nine of his most famous movies (including *Morocco* and *Shanghai Express*). Yet the appearance of Furthman's name in the credits of such Howard Hawks films as *Only Angels Have Wings, To Have and Have Not, The Big Sleep,* and *Rio Bravo* suggests the reasons for the similar qualities of good-bad-girl glamour in the roles played by Dietrich and Bacall and in other von Sternberg and Hawks heroines, and also in the Jean Harlow and Constance Bennett roles in the movies he wrote for *them.* Furthman, who has written about half of the most entertaining movies to come out of Hollywood (Ben Hecht wrote most of the other half), isn't even listed in new encyclopedias of the film. David Newman and Robert Benton may be good enough to join this category of unmentionable men who do what the directors are glorified for. The Hollywood writer is becoming a ghostwriter. The writers who succeed in the struggle to protect their identity and their materials by becoming writer-directors or writer-producers soon become too rich and powerful to bother doing their own writing. And they rarely have the visual sense or the training to make good movie directors.

Anyone who goes to big American movies like *Grand Prix* and *The Sand Pebbles* recognizes that movies with scripts like those don't have a chance to be anything more than exercises in technology, and that this is what is meant by the decadence of American movies. In the past, directors used to say that they were no better than their material. (Sometimes they said it when they weren't even up to their material.) A good director can attempt to camouflage poor writing with craftsmanship and style, but ultimately no amount of director's skill can conceal a writer's failure; a poor script, even well directed, results in a stupid movie — as, unfortunately, does a good script poorly directed. Despite the new notion that the direction is everything, Penn can't redeem bad material, nor, as one may surmise from his *Mickey One,* does he necessarily know when it's bad. It is not fair to judge Penn by a film like *The Chase,* because he evidently did not have artistic control over the production, but what happens when he does have control and is working with a poor, pretentious mess of a script is painfully apparent in *Mickey One* — an art film in the worst sense of that term. Though one cannot say of *Bonnie and Clyde* to what degree it shows the work of Newman and Benton and to what degree it shows Penn to "express himself," there are ways of making guesses. As we hear the lines, we can detect the intentions even when the intentions are not quite carried out. Penn is a little clumsy and rather too fancy; he's too much interested in being cinematically creative and artistic to know when to trust the script. *Bonnie and Clyde* could be better if it were simpler. Nevertheless, Penn is a remarkable director when he has something to work with. His most interesting previous work was in his first film, *The Left-Handed Gun* (and a few bits of *The Miracle Worker,* a good movie version of the William Gibson play, which he had also directed on the stage and television). *The Left-Handed Gun* with Paul Newman as an ignorant Billy the Kid in the sex-starved, male-dominated Old West, has the same kind of violent, legendary, nostalgic material as *Bonnie and Clyde*; its script, a rather startling one, was adapted by Leslie Stevens from a Gore Vidal television play. In interviews, Penn makes high, dull sounds — more like a politician than a movie director. But he has a gift for violence, and, despite all the violence in movies, a gift for it is rare. (Eisenstein had it, and Dovzhenko, and Buñuel, but not many others.) There are few memorable violent moments in American movies, but there is one in Penn's first film : Billy's shotgun blasts a man right out of one of his boots; the man falls in the street, but his boot remains upright; a little girl's giggle at the boot is interrupted by her mother slapping her. The mother's slap — the seal of the awareness of horror — says that even children must learn that some things that look funny are not only funny. That slap, saying that only idiots would laugh at pain and death, that a child must develop sensibility, is the same slap that *Bonnie and Clyde* delivers to the woman saying "It's a comedy." In *The Left-Handed Gun,* the slap is itself funny, and yet we suck in our breath; we do not dare to laugh.

Some of the best American movies show the seams of cuts and the confusions of compromises and still hold together, because there is enough energy and spirit to carry the audience over each of the weak episodes to the next good one. The solid intelligence of the writing and Penn's aura of sensitivity help *Bonnie and Clyde* triumph over many poorly directed scenes: Bonnie posing for the photograph with the Texas Ranger, or — the worst sequence — the Ranger getting information out of Blanche Barrow in the hospital The attempt to make the Texas Ranger an old-time villain doesn't work. He's in the tradition of the mustachioed heavy who foreclosed mortgages and pursued heroines in turn-of-the-century plays, and this one-dimensional villainy belongs, glaringly, to spoof. In some cases, I think, the writing and the conception of the scenes are better (potentially, that is) than the way the scenes have been directed and acted. If Gene Hackman's Buck Barrow is a beautifully controlled performance, the best in the film, several of the other players — though they are very good — needed a tighter rein. They act too much. But it is in other ways that Penn's limitations show — in his excessive reliance on meaning-laden close-ups, for one. And it's no wonder he wasn't able to bring out the character of Bonnie in scenes like the one showing her appreciation of the fingernails on the figurine, for in other scenes his own sense of beauty appears to be only a few rungs farther up that same cultural ladder.

The showpiece sequence, Bonnie's visit to her mother (which is a bit reminiscent of Humphrey Bogart's confrontation with his mother, Marjorie Main, in the movie version of *Dead End*), aims for an effect of alienation, but that effect is confused by all the other things attempted in the sequence: the poetic echoes of childhood (which also echo the child sliding down the hill in *Jules and Jim*) and a general attempt to create a frieze from our national

212

past — a poetry of poverty. Penn isn't quite up to it, though he is at least good enough to communicate what he is trying to do, and it is an attempt that one can respect. In 1939, John Ford attempted a similar poetic evocation of the legendary American past in *Young Mr. Lincoln*; this kind of evocation, by getting at how we feel about the past, moves us far more than attempts at historical recreation. When Ford's Western evocations fail, they become languorous; when they succeed, they are the West of our dreams, and his Lincoln, the man so humane and so smart that he can outwit the unjust and save the innocent, is the Lincoln of our dreams, and the Depression of *Bonnie and Clyde* is the Depression of our dreams — the nation in a kind of trance, as in a dim memory. In this sense, the effect of blur is justified, is "right." Our memories *have* become hazy; this is what the Depression has faded into. But we are too conscious of the technical means used to achieve this blur, of the *attempt* at poetry. We are aware that the filtered effects already include our responses, and it's too easy; the lines are good enough so that the stylization wouldn't have been necessary if the scene had been played right. A simple frozen frame might have been more appropriate.

The editing of this movie is, however, the best editing in an American movie in a long time, and one may assume that Penn deserves credit for it along with the editor, Dede Allen. It's particularly inventive in the robberies and in the comedy sequence of Blanche running through the police barricades with her kitchen spatula in her hand. (There is, however, one bad bit of editing: the end of the hospital scene, when Blanche's voice makes an emotional shift without a corresponding change in her facial position.) The quick panic of Bonnie and Clyde looking at each other's faces for the last time is a stunning example of the art of editing.

The end of the picture, the rag-doll dance of death, as the gun blasts keep the bodies of Bonnie and Clyde in motion, is brilliant. It is a horror that seems to go on for eternity, and yet it doesn't last a second beyond what it should. The audience leaving the theater is the quietest audience imaginable.

Still, that woman near me was saying "It's just a comedy" for a little too long, and although this could have been, and probably

213

was, a demonstration of plain old-fashioned insensitivity, it suggests that those who have attuned themselves to the "total" comedy of the last few years may not know when to stop laughing. Movie audiences have been getting a steady diet of "black" comedy since 1964 and *Dr. Strangelove, Or : How I Learned To Stop Worrying and Love the Bomb*. Spoof and satire have been entertaining audiences since the two-reelers; because it is so easy to do on film things that are difficult or impossible in nature, movies are ideally suited to exaggerations of heroic prowess and to the kind of light-hearted nonsense we used to get when even the newsreels couldn't resist the kidding finish of the speeded-up athlete competition or the diver flying up from the water. The targets have usually been social and political fads and abuses, together with the heroes and and the clichés of the just preceding period of film-making. *Dr. Strangelove* opened a new movie era. It ridiculed everything and everybody it showed but concealed its own liberal pieties, thus protecting itself from ridicule. A professor who had told me that *The Manchurian Candidate* was "irresponsible," adding, "I didn't like it — I can suspend disbelief only so far," was overwhelmed by *Dr. Strangelove* : "I've never been so involved. I had to keep reminding myself it was only a movie." *Dr. Strangelove* was clearly intended as a cautionary movie; it meant to jolt us awake to the dangers of the bomb by showing us the insanity of the course we were pursuing. But artists' warnings about war and the dangers of total annihilation never tell us how we are supposed to regain control, and *Dr. Strangelove,* chortling over madness, did not indicate any possibilities for sanity. It was experienced not as satire but as a confirmation of fears. Total laughter carried the day. A new generation enjoyed seeing the world as insane; they *literally* learned to stop worrying and love the bomb. Conceptually, we had already been living with the bomb; now the mass audience of the movies — which is the youth of America — grasped the idea that the threat of extinction can be used to devaluate everything, to turn it all into a joke; and the members of this audience do love the bomb; they love feeling that the worst has happened and the irrational are the sane, because there is the bomb as the proof that the rational are insane. They love the bomb because it intensifies their feelings of hoplessness and powerlessness and innocence. It's only three years since Lewis Mumford was widely acclaimed for saying about *Dr.*

Strangelove that "unless the spectator was purged by laughter he would be paralyzed by the unendurable anxiety this policy, once it were honestly appraised, would produce." Far from being purged, the spectators are paralyzed, but they're still laughing. And how odd it is now to read, "*Dr. Strangelove* would be a silly, ineffective picture if its purpose were to ridicule the characters of our military and political leaders by showing them as clownish monsters — stupid, psychotic, obsessed." From *Dr. Strangelove* it's a quick leap to *MacBird* and to a belief in exactly what it was said we weren't meant to find in *Dr. Strangelove*. It is not war that has been laughed to scorn but the possibility of sane action.

Once something enters mass culture, it travels fast. In the spoofs of the last few years, everything is gross, ridiculous, insane; to make sense would be to risk being square. A brutal new melodrama is called *Point Blank* and it is. So are most of the new movies. This is the context in which *Bonnie and Clyde*, an entertaining movie that has some feeling in it, upsets people — people who didn't get upset even by *Mondo Cane*. Maybe it's because Bonnie and Clyde, by making us care about the robber lovers, has put the sting back into death.

CRITICISM OF *BONNIE AND CLYDE*

Bonnie and Clyde was certainly one of the most popular films of 1967 in terms of box office returns. Its popularity in the United States grew in spite of the critics who at first either ignored the film or berated it for its excessive violence. Critical opinion then divided into two camps, some critics even going so far as to contradict their own or their newspapers' original views. By the time the film reached Britain the Bonnie and Clyde boom was under way, and the critics generally praised the film, condoning its use of violence as a valid part of the story it tells. The following selection of extracts from reviews and critical analyses will give some idea of the diversity of opinion on both sides of the Atlantic.

Crime Wave by Hollis Alpert

I should say at once that filmically *Bonnie and Clyde* represents a high point in the directional work of Arthur Penn; that it is exceedingly well made; that it has an astonishingly good performance by Warren Beatty as Clyde Barrow . . . What is bothersome about the picture is that David Newman and Robert Benton, the writers, aren't able to make clear their own attitudes toward the two criminals. They show the sexual impotence of Clyde, make something Freudian about both his and Bonnie's love for guns, and imply that the depressed economic times have much to do with their brief life of crime; but they also imply that Clyde is a psychopath and would remain one, even after finally achieving sexual satisfaction with Bonnie. Nor are they quite sure whether Bonnie and Clyde are stark figures of tragedy, or merely two wayward kids, caught in a whirlwind they can't control. They lean toward the former but Penn's realistic and at times poetic camera leans toward the latter, and about all one is left with at the end is that crime may be fun for a while, but that it results in literally a dead end.

Extracts from a review which first appeared in the Saturday Review, *5th August, 1967. Reprinted by permission.*

Thudding Home by John Coleman

Flicked around like bloody puppets as too many bullets stitch them to death, a young psychopath and his moll come to one of the most extraordinary ends in cinema. Arthur Penn's *Bonnie and Clyde*, dazzlingly photographed in colour by Burnett Guffey, makes the other violent films this week seem like child's play. And yet the Penn film is sophisticated enough to be the most playful. Clyde Barrow and Bonnie Parker existed, dreamily taking on three members and becoming the Barrow Gang . . . Bonnie even wrote a doggerel ballad about them which made the papers : they literally publicised themselves into the grave. The film frequently behaves as if it were a homage to that ballad, but rarely less than equivocally . . .

. . . The tone is merry and somehow childlike. An intimation of Robin-Hoodery — the poor, Grant Wood farmer allowed to keep his cash during a bank raid — grips hands with a legendary past. But the killings happen . . . This brilliantly constructed film — surely the hardest to close your eyes on of any to come from America, or elsewhere, in a long time — may err in building up sympathy for its Bonnie and Clyde . . . Afterwards, one asks oneself the difficult questions : most notably, what about a similar treatment . . . applied to another couple who might have made the broadsheets in an earlier age : Brady and Hindley? With considerable hesitation, I would suggest that for once — this once — the aesthetic values of Mr. Penn's film are not there simply to seduce us into accepting untenable or unpleasant moral positions in the cause of entertainment. What that needle-sharp editing of alluring images does is to make sure that we *keep looking* when the foul things happen. Someone might care to find an analogy with the canvasses of Francis Bacon. The attractiveness of shape, focus, colour, makes one attentive, unwilling to duck away. At which point the bullets can really thud home.

Extracts from a review which first appeared in the New Statesman, *on 22nd September, 1967. Reprinted by permission.*

Bonnie and Clyde : Two Reviews by Joseph Morgenstern

In *Bonnie and Clyde* . . . some of the most gruesome carnage since Verdun is accompanied by some of the most gleeful off-screen fiddling since Grand Ole Opry. The effect is ear-catching, to say the least. For those who find killing less than hilarious, the effect is also stomach-turning . . . Were the people in charge of its production actually amused by scores of cops being gunned down or blown up by hand grenades hitting armoured cars? . . .

Whatever the case, the people in charge were not really in charge, and what begins as an engagingly perverse Depression saga . . . transforms itself, willy-nilly, into a squalid shoot-'em-up for the moron trade. Try to imagine *In Cold Blood* being played as a William Inge comedy, including an attempt at lyricism consisting of a slow-motion sequence in which the inert bodies of Bonnie and Clyde, being perforated by the law's lead, rise and fall and pitch and turn with something of the same grace that Vittorio Mussolini must have seen in Ethiopia when he compared bomb bursts to rose petals.

This follow-up review appeared in the next week's issue:

Last week this magazine said that *Bonnie and Clyde* . . . turns into a "squalid shoot-'em-up for the moron trade" because it does not know what to make of its own violence. I am sorry to say I consider that review grossly unfair and regrettably inaccurate. I am sorrier to say I wrote it.

Seeing the film a second time . . . I realised that *Bonnie and Clyde* knows perfectly well what to make of its own violence, and makes a cogent statement with it — that violence is not necessarily perpetrated by shambling cavemen or quivering psychopaths, but may also be the casual easy expression of only slightly aberrated citizens, of jes' folks.

I had become so surfeited and preoccupied by violence in daily life that my reaction was as excessive as the stimulus . . . And yet precisely because *Bonnie and Clyde* combines gratuitous crudities with scene after scene of dazzling artistry . . . it is an ideal laboratory for the study of violence, a subject in which we are all matriculating these days. . . .

The Legend of Bonnie and Clyde by Judith Crist

With *Bonnie and Clyde* Warren Beatty and Arthur Penn firmly establish themselves as one of the most excitingly creative teams in American movie-making. In their second joint effort (their first, *Mickey One,* is still a bit ahead of its audience), the young producer-actor and his director have dealt with an American folk-legend in almost ballad form and triumphed . . .

It is in retrospect that the pathos of Bonnie and Clyde, so much a product of their time and so potentially to be paralleled in ours, is evident — and this evidence provides the particular distinction of what might well have been just another gangster movie . . . Instead Beatty and Penn and their associates have given us a portrait of a pair of displaced young people on the run, catapulted from one atrocity to another by their neurotic sensualities, terrifying in their complete disassociation from humanity, their aspiration to nothing beyond the satisfaction of the moment's whim.

Slowly, almost bucolically, Arthur Penn unfolds the boy-and-girl meeting, underlying the sexuality on Bonnie's part, the introverted bravado on Clyde's. The sordidness of their successes, and the horror of their prankishness, the sadism of their playtime, and the emptiness of their lifetimes is played out, all to the tangy twang of a banjo, against the rolling expanse of a countryside that has little to offer even the non-misfit.

Naturalism — in characters and background — is the mark of this film in its technical perfections. We are so thoroughly saturated with a sense of time and place that we are, paradoxically, compelled to recognize the universality of the theme and its particular contemporary relevance. And this is the triumph of *Bonnie and Clyde.*

Extracts from a review which first appeared in Vogue, September 1967. Copyright © 1969 by the Condé Nast Publications Inc. Reprinted by permission.

Brushing Up the Gangster Film by Tom Milne

Ten years ago the French New Wave stole the American gangster film, dusted it off, gave it a bright new coat of paint — and Hollywood never even noticed. But now Arthur Penn has pinched it back again with *Bonnie and Clyde*. . . . Bonnie Parker and Clyde Barrow, leaders of a gang which terrorised the American south in the early thirties with a plague of bank robberies and killings, have been enshrined in film before, but never quite like this.

The curious fact about these young hoodlums is that they appear to have been fascinated by their own potentiality as legend. Delighted in reading about themselves in the headlines, forever recording their doings with a camera or sending poems to the newspapers, they obviously lived in a fantasy world which only became real when they died . . .

The way leads through riotous comedy . . . but gradually, as the myth grows and so does their self-intoxication, reality catches up with them. Killing piles up on killing; the police draw closer; . . . and one final day, even Bonnie and Clyde are caught unawares . . .

Funny, tender and incredibly savage by turns, and steering a perfect course between all three moods at once, *Bonnie and Clyde* has all the racy rhythm and yearning undertow of a blues. Particular praise should go to the entire cast . . . and to Burnett Guffey, who proves that anything a New Wave cameraman can do, an old Hollywood hand can do better. His colour camerawork on this strange landscape of verdant highways and derelict little Southern towns is quite simply stunning.

Extracts from a review which first appeared in the Observer, *10th September, 1967. Reprinted by permission.*

Bonnie and Clyde by Bosley Crowther

A raw and unmitigated campaign of sheer press agentry has been trying to put across the notion that Warner Brothers' *Bonnie and Clyde* is a faithful representation of the desperado careers of Clyde Barrow and Bonnie Parker . . . It is nothing of the sort. It is a cheap piece of bald-faced slapstick comedy that treats the hideous depredations of that sleezy, moronic pair as though they were as full of fun and frolic as the jazz-age cut-ups in *Thoroughly Modern Millie*.

. . . Such ridiculous, camp-tinctured travesties of the kind of people these desperadoes were . . . might be passed off as candidly commercial movie comedy, nothing more, if the film weren't reddened with blotches of violence of the most grisly sort. Arthur Penn, the aggressive director, has evidently gone out of his way to splash the comedy hold-ups with smears of vivid blood . . .

This blend of farce with brutal killings is as pointless as it is lacking in taste, since it makes no valid commentary upon the already travestied truth. And it leaves an astonished critic wondering just what purpose Mr. Penn and Mr. Beatty think they serve with this strangely antique, sentimental clap trap.

Extracts from a review which first appeared in the New York Times, *14th August, 1967. Reprinted by permission.*

Bonnie and Clyde by Andrew Sarris

Arthur Penn's *Bonnie and Clyde* has been the subject of a Crowther Crusade that makes the 100-Years-War look like a border incident. To use the pages of the *New York Times* for a personal vendetta against a director and actor one doesn't like is questionable enough. To incite the lurking forces of censorship and repression with inflammatory diatribes against violence on the screen is down-right mischievous. Particularly at a time when too many bigots see a golden opportunity to lash back at the Negro with the fake rhetoric of law and order . . . It is much easier (and cheaper) to imply that there is some link between violent movies and violence in the streets than to eradicate the slums.

The late Jimmy Walker showed more common sense when he observed that no girl ever got into trouble reading a book. Similarly, the most depraved movie ever made is a relatively restraining influence as far as physical violence is concerned . . .

Bonnie and Clyde is nothing if not sensuous about violence. Perhaps lyrical would be closer to the mark. Arthur Penn was trying for nothing less than folk tragedy in this saga of a gunhappy couple in the thirties. I thought the subject was handled more movingly some years ago in an obscure movie called *Gun Crazy* (directed by Joseph H. Lewis). The trouble with *Bonnie and Clyde* is that it oscillates between the distancing of period legend and the close-ups of contemporary psychology.

Penn is characteristically good with the scenes calling for physical exhuberance and sustained hysteria . . . Unfortunately, Penn's form, too much a thing of parts, is closer to pathos than to tragedy, and half-baked pathos at that. Still, much of the film is so strikingly original, so unexpectedly funny and endearing that the slanders in the *Times* emerge as exercises in dull spite.

The Village Voice, *24th August, 1967. Reprinted by permission.*

ACKNOWLEDGMENTS

Our special thanks are due to David Newman and Robert Benton, Arthur Penn, and Warren Beatty, for the help and co-operation they have given throughout the preparation of this volume.

Acknowledgments and thanks are due to Warner-Seven Arts Inc., for supplying stills, a dialogue continuity and a copy of the original screenplay, and for making available a print of the film; to *Cahiers du Cinéma* for permission to reproduce the interview with Arthur Penn by André Labarthe and Jean-Louis Comolli; to *Cinema* (USA) for permission to reproduce the article by Robert Towne and interviews by Curtis Lee Hanson; to Pauline Kael for permisison to reproduce from her book *Kiss Kiss Bang Bang* the article on *Bonnie and Clyde* which originally appeared in the *New Yorker*.

Further acknowledgements are due to the following for permission to reproduce extracts from articles and reviews; Hollis Alpert and the *Saturday Review*; John Coleman and the *New Statesman*; Judith Crist and the Condé Nast Publications, Inc.; Bosley Crowther and the *New York Times*; Tom Milne and the *Observer Foreign News Desk*; Joseph Morgenstern and *Newsweek,* Inc.; Andrew Sarris and *The Village Voice*.